HOW THE
MILITARY
W
Y
C

DATE			

HOW THE MILITARY WILL HELP YOU PAY FOR COLLEGE

THE HIGH SCHOOL STUDENT'S GUIDE TO ROTC, THE ACADEMIES, AND SPECIAL PROGRAMS

DON M. BETTERTON

Peterson's Guides
Princeton, New Jersey

Copyright © 1985 by Peterson's Guides, Inc.

Printed in the United States of America

10 9 8 7 6 5 4 3 2 1

Library of Congress Cataloging in Publication Data

Betterton, Don M., 1938–
    How the military will help you pay for college.

    1. Soldiers—Education, Non-military—United States.
2. Scholarships—United States. 3. Student aid—United States.
4. Military education—United States. I. Title.
U716.B48 1985   378'.34'0973   85–12409
ISBN 0-87866-362-2

For information about other Peterson's publications, please see the listing at the back of this volume.

Contents

Acknowledgments

Among those who helped with the writing of this book, I first would like to thank my wife, Finn, for her encouragement, advice and countless hours on the word processor. My son Thom also contributed by providing suggestions for design and layout.

In gathering information about the ROTC programs, Colonel Bob Selkis of the Princeton University Army ROTC Unit, Captain Ron Ball of the University of Pennsylvania NROTC Unit, and Captain Ryall Smith from Rutgers Air Force ROTC were patient and knowledgeable answerers of my many questions. Anita Lancaster from the Office of the Assistant Secretary of Defense helped coordinate the review of the manuscript by the military services. Among those in Washington, D.C., the Army's Major Jim Artis was particularly helpful.

In retrospect, the seemingly straightforward job of collecting descriptions of military college aid programs was a much more ambitious project than I had imagined. There are hundreds of different programs—some created by Congressional law, some designed by the Department of Defense, and some run by the individual services. Moreover, the programs are constantly being updated and revised as the military tries to develop the most effective ways to help finance the education of its officers and enlisted servicemembers.

In spite of these complexities, I tried to keep the basic purpose in mind—to put it all in one place, to get it right, and to explain it clearly. Where I've been successful, I readily acknowledge those who have been so helpful. On the other hand I take the responsibility for any errors of fact or interpretation that may have slipped into this manuscript.

Introduction

Today the cost of going to college is quite high, but the value of a college education is even higher. As the United States economy becomes increasingly dependent on technology—in manufacturing, engineering, finance, and communications—your level of skill and your experience become more important. Not only is a college education crucial in enabling you to keep pace with the requirements of a job, it also will mean a higher standard of living for you. Based on a study by the Census Bureau, average lifetime earnings are expected to be $985,000 for someone with a high school diploma compared to $1,400,000 for a college graduate.

While the value of a college education may be somewhat hard to pin down, the cost is all too obvious. For a full-time student entering in the fall of 1985, the average bill for four years is expected to be about $23,000 at a public college and $42,000 at a private institution. Even if you go to college only part-time you will still end up paying a similar amount, although it may be easier on your pocketbook to spread the payments over a longer period of time.

How to come up with the money to pay for such an expense is one of the major dilemmas that nearly every individual or family faces today. There is an extensive nationwide system of financial aid—totaling $17-billion each year—to help students pay for the portion of college costs they can not afford. However, while this "need-based" assistance is quite important, it is directed primarily at students from low-income families who attend college full-time. The focus of military financial aid is quite different. The military programs do not consider need but are based on either a payment for training or a reward for service. This large source of money (about one billion dollars each year) can prove quite helpful in assisting a wide range of students, varying from a typical college undergraduate from a middle-class family to an enlisted servicemember who is independent of family support. The military financial aid programs are by far the largest source of college money that is not based on need.

In *How The Military Will Help You Pay For College* you will learn about the two major ways in which the military provides financial aid.

First, as described in Part I of this book, is college money for officer candidates—tuition assistance and monthly pay in return for a promise by you to serve as an officer in the Army, Navy, Air Force, Marine Corps, Coast Guard, or Merchant

Marine. Most of this money is awarded to high school seniors who go directly to college. The main benefits are free tuition and $100 per month if you are part of the Reserve Officers' Training Corps (ROTC) Scholarship Program or free tuition, room and board plus $500 per month if you enroll at one of the service academies. ROTC Units are located on college campuses and provide military training for a few hours each week. The five service academies—West Point, Annapolis, Air Force Academy, Coast Guard Academy, and Merchant Marine Academy—are military establishments where education and training for the Armed Forces are combined into one. (The Merchant Marine Academy is more accurately a military-*like* civilian academy. It has a close connection to the Navy in that it trains officers to serve aboard privately owned merchant ships and may also commission Naval officers. The financial benefits are similar to those offered by the military service academies.) There also is financial aid for you if you are now in college, through ROTC scholarships for enrolled students or special commissioning programs.

The second category of major military aid program, as described in Part II, is for enlisted servicemembers. This takes the form of tuition aid and monthly payments given as a "fringe benefit" in return for serving in the military. If you are thinking of postponing your college plans and joining the military first, knowledge of these sources of aid can be an important part of your decision process. While serving on active duty you can receive credit both for learning a military skill and for going to college during off-duty hours. After you have completed your obligated service you can use the money you've saved under the New GI Bill to attend college as a civilian. The military also provides assistance to enlisted servicemembers who qualify for officer training programs.

Before the publication of *How The Military Can Help You Pay For College,* there was no one place where you could go to find out about college money the military pays to officer candidates and enlisted servicemembers. Until now, if you wanted to learn about the requirements and benefits of military college aid, it would have been necessary for you to make separate inquiries at an Army, Navy, Air Force, Marine Corps or Coast Guard recruiting station, to write the admissions office at each of the service academies, or to visit an Army, Navy, or Air Force ROTC unit at a college. This book brings together in one place valuable information about how you might qualify for your share of $1-billion in college money that the military spends each year.

Here are the military financial aid programs that are covered in *How The Military Can Help You Pay For College.*

Officer Training

ROTC Full Tuition Scholarships
Army, Navy/Marine Corps, Air Force

Free Service Academies
West Point, Annapolis, Air Force Academy, Coast Guard Academy, and Merchant Marine Academy

Special Programs
Navy Nuclear Power
Marine Corps Platoon Leaders Class
Air Force College Senior Engineering
Armed Forces Health Professions
Uniformed Services University of the Health Sciences

Enlisted Educational Benefits

In Service
Free college credit for attending military schools and learning
job skills
Tuition reduction for courses taken while off duty

After Service
New GI Bill
College aid for officer candidates

How This Book Is Organized

How The Military Can Help You Pay For College is divided into three parts.
Part I describes programs and benefits for those who choose the direct officer-
training paths, while Part II covers college financial aid programs for enlisted
servicemembers to use while in the service or later.

Part I: Going to College First: College Money for Officer Candidates

Chapter 1, "Going to College and Becoming an Officer—Which Route Is Best?,"
encourages you to look at what the military is like and ask yourself whether you
are the type of person who will fit in with the military lifestyle.

Chapter 2, "Reserve Officers' Training Corps (ROTC)," explains the selection
process, what is expected of you in college, and the types of jobs available after
you are commissioned.

In Chapter 3, "The Service Academies," you learn about this special kind of
education—the admissions process, what life is like at an academy, and career
opportunities.

Chapter 4, "Special Programs," covers routes to a commission separate from
ROTC and the academies.

Chapter 5, "Weighing the Different Options," offers guidelines about which
officer program might be best for you.

Part II: Going into the Military First: College Money for Enlisted Servicemembers

Chapter 6, "Enlisting in the Military—Is It for You?," tells you what it is like
to be an enlisted member of the Armed Forces.

In Chapter 7, "Earning College Credits on Active Duty," you can read about how to advance your college education while you serve in the military.

Chapter 8, "Banking College Money While Enlisted," explains the New GI Bill— who is eligible, how you save money, and how the benefits are paid.

Chapter 9, "Going from Enlisted Servicemember to Officer," describes commissioning programs for enlisted servicemembers.

Part III: Appendixes

Appendix A is a comprehensive list of all colleges that have any kind of ROTC Unit.

Appendixes B, C, and D show, by service, where ROTC Units are located.

Appendix E is a schedule of military pay and benefits.

Appendix F is a height and weight chart for officer candidates.

Points to Keep in Mind

The material in this book is current as of April 1985. It includes information about college programs through the 1986–87 academic year. It describes the New GI Bill, which became effective on July 1, 1985. However, owing to the nature of these programs, the information is subject to change.

This book is not intended to be the final authority on rules and regulations nor to give you complete details on every option. After you have a better feel for which program meets your needs, you should ask for the latest official publication or visit a recruiting station.

When the time comes for you to attend college (unless you go to one of the academies), you may find you are short of money even though you have tuition benefits from the military. Should this occur, remember there are other types of financial aid available. To learn more about sources of aid beyond what the military offers, check with your high school guidance counselor or a college financial aid officer.

PART I

Going to College First: Scholarship Programs for High School Seniors

This part of *How The Military Can Help You Pay For College* is written primarily for high school students who plan to go to college before serving in the military and who want to know more about the two main sources of military scholarships: tuition assistance at any one of the hundreds of colleges that sponsor ROTC or a free education at one of the five service academies—West Point, Annapolis (which includes preparation for the Marine Corps), the Air Force Academy, the Coast Guard Academy, or the Merchant Marine Academy. The ROTC scholarships are explained in greatest detail, not merely because they are considerably more numerous than openings at the academies, but also because there are so many options for you to be aware of.

Part I will also be of value to you if you are now in college and are unaware of the different types of scholarships the military has for enrolled undergraduates— money that can be crucial in helping you finish the last two or three years of an academic program you have already started. Chapter 2 discusses the 2- or 3-year "in-college" ROTC scholarships that do not receive the same degree of publicity as the 4-year ROTC scholarships or the service academies. As a result, these 2- and 3-year awards are often overlooked by college students who need financial aid and are interested in becoming military officers. There is also a chapter entitled "Special Programs" which tells you about other sources of college aid such as the Navy's Nuclear Power Program and the Marine Corps Platoon Leaders Class.

The following chapters on officer programs are intended to give you the information you need to compare your abilities and preferences with the requirements of the military service that is offering the scholarship. This should benefit you by clearing up any misconceptions you may have about what options are available.

1

The military services will also benefit if students have a better understanding of these programs before they apply. The result—a better match between student and service—should produce more satisfied officers and reduce the attrition that comes from a misunderstanding of program rules and regulations.

There is a further reason to give both high school and college students an easy-to-understand "roadmap" to officer training programs. The idea of serving as a military officer has become an attractive opportunity for thousands of college students. The appeal of the military service has changed a great deal in recent years and many potential college graduates look upon a military tour of duty as a good way to learn management skills, exercise leadership, and serve their country at the same time. Even if you decide not to pursue a military career and to leave the service after four or five years, the experience you've gained can prove to be very valuable, in terms of both your personal growth and your attractiveness to employers who look favorably upon job applicants who have prior military service.

1

Going to College and Becoming an Officer—Which Route Is Best?

Participating in ROTC, attending a service academy, or enrolling in a special program for military commissioning not only allows you to become an officer but also provides sources of financial aid that can enable you to attend a college that you might otherwise be unable to afford. The military teaches you to become an officer and pays you to learn at the same time. Your "rate of pay" can be viewed as the extent to which your education is subsidized.

The Services and Their Programs

There are five military services—the Army, Navy, Air Force, Marine Corps, and Coast Guard—that have the responsibility for defending the United States in time of war. Each of these carries out its basic mission through an organization in which officers direct the work of enlisted personnel. Although it is possible to become a military officer by attending an Officer Candidate School after graduation from college, the vast majority of officers are trained while they are in college, by participating in ROTC, attending a service academy, or taking advantage of a special program like the Marine Corps Platoon Leaders Class. In four of the services—Army, Navy, Air Force, and Marine Corps—both ROTC and academy options are available. (A future Marine Corps officer joins Naval ROTC or attends Annapolis.) The Coast Guard does not sponsor an ROTC program, instead concentrating its college military training at the Coast Guard Academy. The nonmilitary Merchant Marine, although closely allied with the Navy, provides its own officers from the Merchant Marine Academy; it has no ROTC option. Officer candidates in the Army, Air Force, and Coast Guard are called cadets, while potential Navy, Marine Corps, and Merchant Marine officers are referred to as midshipmen.

Is an Officer Training Program Right for Me?

The fundamental purpose of military scholarship programs is to give money to college students as they go through officer training in return for a commitment to serve in the Armed Forces. Through this method of attracting outstanding young men and women, the military hopes to produce an "entry-level" officer who is well educated—in terms of both academics and the workings of the military itself. You should not try for one of these programs if you have moral or religious reservations about serving your country as a military officer. Also, although the financial benefits may be very important, you should not apply if money is the only reason the program appeals to you. In balance with the financial benefits should be the feeling that you will seriously consider becoming an officer, you will undertake military training with a positive attitude, and you will be open-minded about your future plans. The typical applicant is a young man or woman who is willing to serve at least four or five years as an officer in return for four years of a good education at little or no cost.

The First Test: Am I the "Military Type"?

The question of whether or not you are cut out to be in the military is an important one you need to answer at the outset. Rather than trying to picture yourself at age 22 as a second lieutenant or ensign, or at age 42 as a senior military officer, instead look at yourself now. Take a personal inventory and think about what you are like, how you relate to others, and what kind of organization you want to be part of.

Are you energetic, intelligent, well-rounded, and somewhat athletic? Do you organize your time well? Are you a serious student who gets good grades in precollege courses and has an aptitude for math and science?

Are you outgoing and do you work well with others, both one-on-one and in larger groups? Do you willingly take direction from others? Do you enjoy leadership positions?

Can you deal with a structured and disciplined environment? Do you have strong feelings of patriotism? Are you willing to defend your country in wartime?

If you have answered yes to most of these questions, you possess the kinds of characteristics the military services are interested in, and, even more important, you may be the type of person who can adapt to the military's particular lifestyle. The military is similar to other large businesses that seek to hire employees that will fit well with the mission and style of the company. While there are many different types of military officers—ranging from the quiet intellectual to the outgoing athlete—there nevertheless is a set of generally accepted characteristics that hold true for the average officer. These include a mixture of certain personal traits along with a willingness to be part of a large and very structured organization.

The Second Test: What Kind of Military Training Might Be Best for Me?

Assuming your personal inventory showed you are at least somewhat the "military type," the next step is to see how you match up with the programs the different services offer. As a starting point, ask yourself which of the following most closely describes your present outlook.

1. I have firsthand knowledge of the military service. I can picture myself as an officer, perhaps even a career officer. I have experience with discipline, in both taking and giving orders. While in college I plan to major in science or engineering. A top-quality education at very low cost is quite important to me.
2. Military service is of interest to me. I have little direct experience but I am willing to learn more. I'm not sure whether I'm ready to immerse myself completely in a military environment as a college student. I've done well in math and science but I may want to major in another field. I can look forward to the prospect of four years of service as an officer before deciding whether to stay on. A full-tuition scholarship is appealing and would widen my range of college possibilities.
3. I don't have a negative attitude towards the military but it's not something I know very much about. I might like to give it a look. I'm not sure about studying math and science, as I think my interests may be in other areas. I'm concerned about paying for college but my parents could see me through at least one or two years.
4. I don't think I'm the military type but I really haven't thought much about it. I doubt I would go for the discipline. I certainly would not want to commit myself to anything until I've been in college for a few years and can see which way I want to head. I could possibly see myself serving in the military if I could get duty which would match with my academic interests. I could use a scholarship but I plan to try to seek help through other kinds of financial aid programs.

Which paragraph or paragraphs most nearly describe your attitude towards the military? There is a general correlation between the numbers above and the suggested courses of action below.

1. Think seriously about competing for an appointment to a service academy.
2. Plan to enter the ROTC national four-year scholarship competition.
3. Join an ROTC unit in college and see what the military is like. Scholarship opportunities are available if you decide to stay on.
4. Don't get involved with a military program yet, but keep the service in mind for possible entrance after two years of college—either the two-year ROTC option or one of the special programs described in Chapter 4.

In trying to decide whether the military is right for you, it would be wise to avoid extreme discepancies in these two lists. If, for example, you feel description number 4 is accurate, it is highly unlikely that a military academy or even the four-year ROTC scholarship is the right program for you. It would be far wiser to choose the third or fourth course of action, since later on, after you are enrolled in college, you could easily find that some aspects of the military fit with your academic interests and that the military lifestyle is something you can adapt to. On the other hand, if you feel description number 1 suits you, it is worth your while to pursue either the service academy or ROTC scholarship option when you graduate from high school. If you are this far along in your thinking about a possible future in the military, you might as well try for an officer training program as part of your college experience and take advantage of both the financial benefits the services offer and the head start you will get towards a possible military career.

High School Preparation

To improve your chances to win a four-year ROTC scholarship or receive an appointment to a service academy, you should be enrolled in a precollege program in your high school. With the exception of the Coast Guard Academy and the Merchant Marine Academy (their requirements are shown in Chapter 3), the services don't require you to take specific subjects. However, the Army, Navy, Air Force, and Marine Corps all state that a good high school curriculum is quite important and suggest the following:

English	4 years
Math (through Calculus)	4 years
Foreign Language	2 years
Laboratory Science	2 years
American History	1 year

It is also important for you to be an active member of your school community, and, if possible, to hold leadership positions in extracurricular activities and sports. If your high school has a Junior ROTC unit, you should join the detachment to improve your chances of being selected for an ROTC scholarship or admitted to a service academy. The services also look with favor upon students who are involved in community and church activities and who find the time to hold down a part-time job.

SAT AND ACT

You should be prepared to take the SAT or ACT for entrance into the academies or most other colleges. These tests are used by many college admissions offices as one of the measures of the academic potential of a prospective college student. The SAT (Scholastic Aptitude Test) is sponsored by the College Board and is given about six times a year at a number of locations throughout the country. It consists of a math section and a verbal section, with scores ranging from 200 to 800 on each. The ACT (developed by the American College Testing Program) covers four areas—math, English, social studies, and natural sciences—with scores ranging from 1 to 36 on each. You take whichever test—SAT or ACT—is required by the colleges to which you are applying; the military scholarship programs will accept results from either one.

Profile of a Successful Candidate

John or Jane Doe, the typical winner of a four-year ROTC scholarship or a service academy appointment, exhibits certain kinds of characteristics. (We'll use John for convenience's sake.)

John is following a curriculum that includes four years of English, four years of math, three or four years of a foreign language, two years of laboratory science, and two years of history. Some of the courses are at the honors level. He is maintaining a B+ average and ranks in the top 15% of his class. On the SAT, he received a 560 verbal and 640 math. (If he took the ACT his composite score would be 27.)

John is a member of the National Honor Society. He holds an office in the student government and is a candidate for Boys State. John is involved in other school activities and has a leadership position on the student newspaper while being a member of the debate panel and math club. He participates in varsity athletics and is a co-captain of the basketball team.

John's teachers say he is one of the top all-around students in his class, and he contributes positively to the school environment. He is described as intelligent, industrious, well-organized, self-confident, concerned, and emotionally mature.

John is also active outside school. He works four hours each week in a local drugstore and volunteers some of his time on weekends to help in the town's aid-to-the-handicapped program.

The service believes that a person like John Doe will do well in college—in both academic and military training—and also will have a high probability of becoming a productive officer after graduation.

Common Characteristics of the Officer Training Programs

OFFICER PAY AND BENEFITS

As a military officer you will be paid the standard rate for all members of the Armed Forces based on rank and length of service. In addition to your salary there are significant fringe benefits such as free medical care and a generous retirement plan. (See Appendix E for details.)

THE DIFFERENCE BETWEEN A REGULAR AND A RESERVE OFFICER

In the descriptions of the various officer training programs, there are references to "Regular" and "Reserve" officers. You should be aware of the differences between the two designations.

When you are commissioned as a Regular officer, you are on a career path in the military. In the event you choose not to serve the full twenty years, you must write a letter asking if you can resign your commission. Such requests are normally accepted once you have completed your minimum service obligation. If you plan to make the military your career, it is a definite advantage to be a Regular officer. Among ROTC scholarship recipients, virtually all Navy midshipmen, about 25% of the Army cadets, and a small number of Air Force cadets are given Regular commissions.

As a Reserve officer, you contract for a specific term, for example, four years of active duty in the case of an ROTC scholarship. Nearly all Air Force ROTC second lieutenants are in this category along with about 75% of Army ROTC graduates. If you want to remain on active duty after your initial obligation, you must request to sign on for a second term. It is possible to serve for twenty years as a Reserve officer although nearly all career officers are Regulars, either by initial designation or by "integration" (switching from Reserve to Regular).

There is another category of Reserve officers—those who are assigned to the Reserve Forces rather than to the active-duty military. About 50% of the officers who are commissioned through the Army ROTC are given orders to the National Guard or Army Reserve. After attending the Basic Course for six months, these officers join the Reserve Forces to finish their obligated service as "Weekend Warriors." In this case, the time commitment is seven and one half years in the Reserves, the first five and one half years involving drills one weekend per month and two weeks of active duty each year. During the last two years of obligated service, these officers are transferred to inactive Reserve status in which drills are not required.

WOMEN OFFICERS

Each of the officer training programs mentioned in Chapters 2, 3, and 4 are open to women. With the exception of differences in height and weight standards (see Appendix F) and lower minimums on the physical fitness test, the eligibility rules, benefits, and obligations are the same for women as they are for men.

There is, however, a difference between men and women when it comes to duty assignments. By Act of Congress, women are prohibited from serving in combat units. To what extent this law restricts the types of jobs you can choose varies from service to service. The Navy and Marine Corps have the highest percentage of positions classified as combat-related, the Army and Air Force have somewhat fewer, and the Coast Guard is least restrictive, opening virtually all its jobs to men and women alike.

Regardless of the limits imposed on the services by the combat restrictions for women, there has been considerable improvement in the last 10 years in the position of women within the military. Depending on the service, women make up between 8% and 20% of the officers and they are gradually but steadily moving into the higher ranking positions.

MEDICAL REQUIREMENTS

Each candidate for an ROTC scholarship or an academy appointment must pass a medical examination. These exams are coordinated by the Department of Defense Medical Examination Review Board. Even if you apply for more than one type of scholarship you will only have to take one physical. Each individual service coordinates with the Medical Examination Review Board the specific medical standards it wants for its own programs.

The general rule about medical standards is that they vary considerably and they can be quite complicated. In spite of this, it is worthwhile for you to have at the outset an idea of the general medical requirements, particularly the eyesight and height and weight rules. If you read this information now, you will avoid applying to a program in which you fall short of a basic standard. Each of the program descriptions in Chapters 2 and 3 includes a section on medical requirements. The descriptions are not intended to be all-inclusive but to give you helpful guidance. Also keep in mind that medical standards change periodically and some of them may be waived under certain conditions.

Chapter **2**

Reserve Officers' Training Corps (ROTC)

The predominant way for a college student to become a military officer is through the Reserve Officers' Training Corps program: about 15,600 officers come out of ROTC programs each year, while the academies produce 2,950 officers. ROTC is offered by the Army, Navy, and Air Force, with Marine Corps option students participating in Navy ROTC. (The Coast Guard and Merchant Marine do not sponsor ROTC programs.)

Each service that has an ROTC program signs an agreement with a number of colleges to "host" a unit on their campuses. The Army has 314 detachments, the Navy 64, and the Air Force 151. Each of these units has a commanding officer who supervises a staff of active duty officers and enlisted servicemembers who conduct the military training of cadets and midshipmen. This instruction includes regular class periods in which military science is taught, as well as longer "drill" sessions in which ROTC students concentrate on developing leadership qualities through military formations, physical fitness, and field exercises.

It is not necessary for you to attend a college that hosts a unit to participate in ROTC. In addition to the 529 ROTC detachments, there are another 1,810 cross-enrollment opportunities. The Army has 1,034, the Navy 118, and the Air Force 658. You may attend any one of the colleges that has a cross-enrollment contract and participate in ROTC at the host institution, provided you are accepted into the unit and you are able to arrange your schedule so you have time to commute to the ROTC classes and drill sessions. (The Army also has 107 extension centers—small branches of host colleges that provide an additional way to participate in Army ROTC.)

As a member of an ROTC unit you are a part-time cadet or midshipman. You are required to wear a uniform and adhere to military discipline when you attend an ROTC class or drill, but not otherwise. Since this involvement only averages about four hours per week, most of the time you will follow the same lifestyle as a typical college student. You must realize, however, that while you are an undergraduate you will be trained to become an officer when you graduate from college. You therefore will have a number of obligations and responsibilities your classmates will not face. Nevertheless, the part-time nature of your military training is the major difference between participating in ROTC and enrolling at a service academy where you are in a military environment twenty-four hours a day.

In each ROTC unit there are two types of students—scholarship and nonscholarship. Although the focus of this book is on military programs that provide tuition aid, it should be pointed out that you may join an ROTC unit after you get to college even if you don't receive a scholarship. You take the same ROTC courses as a scholarship student and you may major in nearly any subject. You can drop out at any time prior to the start of your junior year. If you continue you will be paid $100 per month for your last two years of college and be required to attend a summer training session between your junior and senior years. Upon graduation you will be commissioned as a second lieutenant or ensign. Your minimum active duty obligation is three years, four years if you are in the Air Force. About 87,000 of the 115,000 students in ROTC are not on scholarship.

If you want to be an ROTC scholarship student, the most important program is the four-year tuition scholarship available to high school seniors based on a national competition. Each year approximately 5,700 winners are selected (1,500 Army, 2,200 Navy, and 2,000 Air Force) from about 30,000 applicants. Recipients of Navy and Air Force four-year ROTC scholarships may attend either a host or cross-enrollment college. Currently the Army does not permit four-year scholarship winners to cross-enroll; they must attend a host college.

In return for the ROTC scholarship you must serve four years on active duty, unless you choose a branch of the service (such as aviation) that requires extended training. After you accept the scholarship, you have a one-year grace period before you incur a military obligation. Prior to beginning your sophomore year, you may simply withdraw from the program. If you drop out after that time you may be (1) permitted to leave without penalty, (2) ordered to active duty as an enlisted servicemember, or (3) required to repay your financial aid. The military will choose one of these three options depending on the circumstances of your withdrawal.

Should you decide to try for a four-year ROTC scholarship, it is important that, separate from the ROTC competition itself, you apply to a college to which you can bring your ROTC scholarship. Because there is always the possibility you may not be accepted at your first choice, it is a good idea to apply to more than one college with an ROTC affiliation. In the case of Army and Air Force ROTC scholarships, both of which require you to major in a specified area, you also need to be admitted to the particular program for which the scholarship is offered. For example, if you win an Air Force ROTC scholarship designated for an engineering major, in addition to gaining entrance to college as a whole, you must be accepted into the engineering program.

While the majority of new ROTC scholarships are four-year awards given to high school seniors, each service sets aside scholarships for students who are already enrolled in college and who want to try for this kind of military financial aid for their last two or three years. These "in-college" scholarships are a rapidly growing area within the ROTC program. The services are finding that they can do a better job of selecting officer candidates after observing one or two years of college performance than they can if they choose from among high school seniors. Furthermore, of interest to applicants is the fact that the selection rate is quite a bit higher for the two- and three-year awards than it is for the four-year national scholarship. (For example, in a recent year the Air Force ROTC accepted 37% of its candidates for four-year awards and 63% for two- and three-year awards.)

Most of these in-college scholarships are given to students who join an ROTC unit without a scholarship and then decide to try for a tuition grant. Since a cadet or midshipman takes the same ROTC courses whether on scholarship or not, it makes good sense for those who are not receiving aid to apply for an in-college award.

Even if you have not been a member of an ROTC Unit during your first two years in college, it is possible to receive a two-year scholarship provided you apply by the spring of your sophomore year. If you win a two-year scholarship, you will go to a military summer school where you will be taught the equivalent of the first two years of ROTC courses. You then join the ROTC unit for your junior and senior years. (There are also limited opportunities for non-ROTC members to try for a three-year in-college scholarship; interested students should check with an ROTC Unit.)

If you receive a two- or three-year scholarship, your active duty obligation is four years. Moreover, you will not have the one-year grace period available to four-year scholarship winners to decide if they want to remain in ROTC. You must make up your mind whether or not you want to stay when you attend your first military science class as a scholarship student.

Unlike the service academies, you may be married and still receive an ROTC scholarship. The benefits are the same regardless of whether you are married or single.

In summary, there are four ways to participate in ROTC:

1. as a winner of a four-year scholarship for high school seniors
2. as a recipient of a two- or three-year scholarship for ROTC members who are not initially on scholarship
3. by receiving an in-college scholarship (usually for two years) designated for students who have not yet joined an ROTC Unit
4. as a non-scholarship student

This table shows the number of students currently in various Army, Navy and Air Force ROTC programs.

	Army ROTC	Navy ROTC	Air Force ROTC
Total number of students enrolled	76,000	11,200	27,800

	Army ROTC	Navy ROTC	Air Force ROTC
Number of scholarships in effect	12,000	8,000	8,000
Four-year awards	4,500	7,200	6,500
Two- and three-year awards	7,500	800	1,500
Number of officers produced each year	10,700	1,600	3,300

ARMY ROTC

The evolution of the Army is intertwined with much of the history of the United States itself. There was an Army at Valley Forge under George Washington, at Gettysburg commanded by General Meade, during World War I in Europe, and in World War II in many parts of the world. The U.S. Army, with its traditional branches of infantry, artillery, and armor, has long had the responsibility of providing land forces to defend the United States in time of war. The modern Army consists of about 18 branches, with assignments ranging from missile expert to helicopter pilot to budget officer.

The United States Military Academy, commonly called West Point, was the only source of Regular Army officers for many years after its founding in 1802. By 1900, a number of colleges offered a military training program, but it was not until the time of World War I that Congress established Army ROTC in order to create a way that young men could become Army officers directly upon graduation from civilian colleges.

Today, with Army ROTC participation possible at 1,454 different colleges, more than 75% of all Army second lieutenants come from the ROTC program. In fact, Army ROTC provides about twice as many Regular (career-oriented) second lieutenants as West Point. If you are interested in an Army career, West Point appears to offer a small advantage over ROTC, as its graduates are more numerous among the highest ranking officers. But overall the differences are fairly minor, and each year more and more ROTC graduates are advancing to the highest levels of the Army.

The Army ROTC is the oldest and largest of the ROTC programs. The founding of Army ROTC in its present form dates to 1919 when, at the close of World War I, units were established at 125 colleges across the nation. Today there are 314 colleges that host Army ROTC units and 106 extension centers of these host colleges. In addition, there are 1,034 colleges that have cross-enrollment agreements which allow a student to attend one of these colleges and commute to a host institution to participate in ROTC. A list of colleges with Army ROTC is found in Appendix B.

Under current rules, to receive the Army four-year scholarship, you must be enrolled at one of the 314 host colleges; you are not permitted to cross-enroll or to go to college at an extension center. You may, however, attend one of the cross-enrollment or extension center colleges and compete for a two- or three-year scholarship. (The Army is currently evaluating whether to broaden the college options for four-year scholarship holders by adding some of the cross-enrollment or extension center colleges.)

Although virtually all Army scholarship recipients attend four-year colleges, there are six military junior colleges where you can take the first two years of ROTC courses provided you are prepared to transfer to an approved college to get your bachelor's degree.

Army ROTC offers a limited number of its four-year scholarships to high school students who want to attend a historically black college. This option is called the Quality Enrichment Program and there are 21 colleges (for example, Tuskegee, Howard, and Morgan State) participating.

As might be expected, since the Army has considerably more ROTC host units than the Navy and Air Force, as well as the most colleges with cross-enrollment agreements, it also offers the most scholarships and produces the largest number of officers. For 1985–86, there are 12,000 Army scholarships, of which approximately 1,500 will be new four-year scholarships given to students entering college as freshmen. Counting cadets who are already enrolled, there are about 4,500 four-year scholarships in effect in any given year. The other 7,500 are used as in-college scholarships for either two or three years. The large scope of the Army ROTC program is important, since with an Army scholarship there is a wider range of possibilities about where to attend college, and a greater number of two- and three-year scholarships for which to compete.

The Army ROTC (like the Air Force) uses academic quotas in awarding scholarships. In Army ROTC, 30% of the scholarship recipients must be engineers. The other 70% can major in either the sciences or nontechnical fields.

Perhaps the most distinctive aspect of the Army ROTC program is its practice of assigning a number of its second lieutenants to the Reserve Forces, consisting of the National Guard and Army Reserve. This means that for many AROTC scholarship recipients, the only active duty requirement will be to attend a six-month officer's Basic Course before joining a Reserve unit for five and one half years of service as a "Weekend Warrior." (Currently neither the Navy or Air Force ROTC offers this alternative—a newly commissioned officer in either of these two services must serve a minimum of four years on active duty.) If you are the type of person who would like to limit the time you spend on active duty and instead begin to pursue your civilian career plans, this special Reserve commission can be a very desirable option. On the other hand, if you place a high priority on being assured four years of active duty, this unique characteristic of Army ROTC may be a disadvantage. Based on its manpower needs, each year the Department of the Army decides how many officers will be assigned to the active duty Army and how many will go to the Reserve Forces. At present about 50% of AROTC graduates are earmarked for the National Guard or Army Reserve.

THE FOUR-YEAR SCHOLARSHIP FOR HIGH SCHOOL SENIORS

Scholarship Benefits

Winners of the four-year scholarship receive:

1. tuition and fees
2. an allowance for books
3. $100 per month for the academic year
4. a travel allowance from your home to college to begin your freshman year
5. payment during summer training at a rate of about $400 per month
6. uniforms
7. free flights on military passenger aircraft when there is space available.

Scholarship Obligations

In return for the scholarship you are required to:

1. study in the academic area in which the scholarship is offered and meet your college's requirements for a bachelor's degree
2. enlist in the Army Reserve, enroll in an Army ROTC Unit, and complete the four-year Military Science program
3. complete one semester of a foreign language
4. attend one six-week summer training period
5. upon graduation, accept a commission as an officer in either the Regular Army or the Reserve Forces
6. serve at least four years on active duty, unless you are assigned to the Reserve Forces, in which case your active duty obligation can be as short as six months.

Application and Selection

ELIGIBILITY STANDARDS

To receive a four-year scholarship you must:

1. be a United States citizen
2. graduate from high school but not be enrolled in college
3. be at least 17 years old but no more than 21
4. be accepted by a college with an Army ROTC unit on campus
5. plan to pursue a specific course of study
6. be of good moral character and have no personal convictions against serving in the military.

THE SELECTION PROCESS

You will be asked to fill out a detailed application and submit either SAT or ACT scores. Selection of finalists will be based on:

1. minimum SAT of 850 (combined math and verbal) or minimum ACT of 17
2. high school academic standing
3. extracurricular participation with emphasis on leadership roles and athletics.

Finalists are also required to:

1. have a personal interview with an Army officer
2. pass a medical exam
3. pass a physical fitness test.

INTENDED COURSE OF STUDY IN COLLEGE

In awarding its four-year scholarships, the Army is looking for students who possess certain academic skills. Because many of the positions in the modern Army are technical in nature, there is an emphasis on engineering and science backgrounds. Below you will see the breakdown of scholarship winners according to their intended majors in college. As you can see, the chances of being selected are highest for those who expect to study in engineering, physical science, and business. They are considerably lower for those interested in social science, nursing, humanities, prelaw and premedicine.

Engineering	30%
Physical Science	25%
Business	20%
Social Science	10%
Nursing	7%
Other (humanities, prelaw, premed)	8%

MEDICAL REQUIREMENTS

If you become a finalist, you must pass a comprehensive medical exam. Here are some of the important standards.

1. *Height and Weight*
   Weight must be proportional to height. (See the chart in Appendix F.)

Height Range	Men	5'0" to 6'8"
	Women	4'10" to 6'0"

2. *Eyesight*
   Distant and near vision can be correctable to 20/20 but there are limitations on muscle balance and refractive error. Color vision: ability to distinguish between vivid red and vivid green.

3. *Hearing*

Allowable decibel loss varies from 25 in low frequencies to 45 at high frequencies.

4. *Allergies*

No severe hay fever. No symptoms of asthma since age 12.

5. *Heart*

Normal heartbeat. No hypertension or history of cardiovascular problems.

6. *Teeth*

Numerous unfilled cavities may be a cause for disqualification.

Note: You should take care of any correctable deficiencies before you report for a physical.

PHYSICAL FITNESS STANDARDS

Before you can be awarded a scholarship, you must demonstrate your physical fitness by achieving satisfactory performance in the kneeling basketball throw, standing broad jump, 300-yard shuttle run, and pull-ups (for men) or flexed arm hang (for women).

SELECTION TIMETABLE

Early Selection

If you want to be a candidate for early selection you should begin getting ready during the spring of your junior year in high school.

June	Latest date to take SAT or ACT
August 15	ROTC application deadline
November	Army notifies winners subject to passing the medical exam

Regular Selection

December 1	Application deadline
December	Latest date to take SAT or ACT
Fall/early winter	Apply to the colleges of your choice
Winter	Take the medical exam and physical fitness test
March	Army notifies winners

Keep in mind that you must be admitted both to an Army host college and into the academic program you specified on your ROTC application. For example, if the Army approves your scholarship for study in engineering, your college must accept you into its engineering school.

Attending College

YOUR OBLIGATION TO THE ARMY UNIT

You will be required to take four years of Military Science courses, including both classroom and drill sessions. In class you will learn about the Army from books; in drill periods you will learn by doing—through marching, map-reading, physical fitness activities, and field exercises.

In a typical program, you will enroll during the first two years in the Basic Course for one and a half hours per week of class time. The Basic Course consists of an introduction to the Army organization, military concepts, and management skills. In your junior and senior years, you will take the Advanced Course for two and a half hours per week. The Advanced Course focuses on military history, tactics, military justice, and issues affecting the modern Army. The drill sessions continue for about two hours each week for your entire four years. Your total time commitment runs about three to four hours per week during the freshman and sophomore years, increasing to four or five hours per week during the junior and senior years. Depending on the college you attend, the amount of academic credit you receive for your ROTC classes will vary. On average, you will receive academic credit for about half of your military science courses.

In addition, usually once each semester, there will be field training, an exercise in which classroom principles are tested in a military environment. You may also participate in voluntary activities, such as a drill team or social club.

YOUR ACADEMIC PROGRAM IN COLLEGE

You must pass a one-semester course in a foreign language. You are also required to continue to study in the academic area you specified when you were selected as a scholarship recipient. Any change in major must be approved by the Army or you face possible loss of your scholarship. While it will not be difficult to switch majors within the same field (for example going from chemistry to physics), you probably will have to reapply for your scholarship if you transfer to a different course of study.

SUMMER TRAINING

Between your junior and senior years you will attend an Army Advanced Camp for six weeks. You will be there with hundreds of other cadets from colleges in your ROTC region. At summer camp you will learn about the different branches that comprise the Army so you can get a better idea of which one you would like to serve in after graduation. You also will be evaluated for your potential as a future Army officer in areas such as leadership, marksmanship, and land navigation.

Nursing students attend a special summer training session at an Army medical facility.

GRADUATE SCHOOL OPPORTUNITIES

Although all three services prefer that newly commissioned officers proceed directly to active duty, the Army is fairly open-minded when it comes to allowing its officers to attend graduate school. Subject to Army approval, there are two ways you can do this. First, you can simply defer reporting to active duty and attend graduate school as a civilian at your own expense. Second, you can be selected for a special graduate program in which you attend college as a salaried officer with your tuition expenses paid by the Army. In this category there are advanced education for the health professions and a technical enrichment program for other specialties. If you don't go to graduate school after college, and you decide to stay in the Army after your first tour of duty, in all likelihood you will have additional opportunities to pursue an advanced degree.

Active Duty Requirements

LENGTH OF SERVICE

If you are commissioned as a Regular Army officer, or a Reserve officer assigned to the active duty Army, your minimum obligation is four years. If you are commissioned as a Reserve officer with an assignment to the National Guard or Army Reserves, you will serve six months of active duty followed by seven and a half years in the Reserve Forces. As a member of a Ready Reserve unit, you attend drills one weekend per month and go on two weeks of active duty each year. During your last two years, you are placed in Standby Reserve and are not required to attend drills. If you decide to enter Army aviation, your service obligation is four years after approximately one year of flight training. Whenever the Army pays for your graduate school, your active duty obligation is extended, usually by an additional year for each year of school.

TYPES OF JOBS

During your senior year you will be given the opportunity to select the branch of the Army in which you would like to serve after you are commissioned as a second lieutenant. Nearly all cadets are assigned to one of their first three choices. When you report to active duty you will work as a supervisor and manager of resources (both people and equipment) in a position of leadership and responsibility. Second lieutenants who go to graduate school before reporting for active duty are likely to become specialists, such as physicians or lawyers.

The branches you may request and what they include are:

Air Defense Artillery: air defense weapons systems including missiles, fire control equipment, radar, and computers.

Armor: tanks and armored reconnaissance vehicles.

Aviation: helicopters and fixed-wing airplanes.

Corps of Engineers: Army construction projects, including electric power production, buildings, highways, airfields, and bridges.

Field Artillery: guns, missiles, rockets and related weapons; also support equipment such as radars, range finders, and survey instruments.

Infantry: rifles, mortars, antitank missiles, personnel carriers, vehicle-mounted guns, and fire control equipment.

Chemical Corps: chemical, biological and radiological activities, decontamination, and smoke production.

Military Intelligence: information associated with military plans and operations.

Signal Corps: radio and radar receiving and transmitting equipment.

Adjutant General: personnel administration and management.

Finance: pay records, fund accounting, budgets, auditing and statistical analysis.

Ordnance: ammunition and explosives.

Quartermaster Corps: supplies, equipment, and spare parts.

Transportation: passenger and cargo vehicles and boats.

Medical Service: medical, dental, psychological, and social work.

For more information about the four-year Army ROTC scholarship, see your high school guidance counselor, visit an Army ROTC unit on a college campus, or contact:

Army ROTC Scholarships
Fort Monroe, Virginia 23651

Telephone: 804-727-3868

TWO- AND THREE-YEAR SCHOLARSHIPS FOR COLLEGE STUDENTS

If you missed out on the national competition for an Army scholarship while you were in high school, you may still try for tuition assistance if you are enrolled at any of the 1,454 colleges that offer the opportunity to participate in Army ROTC. As a first step you should visit the nearest Army ROTC unit and sign up for the Basic Course. Once enrolled, you are eligible to apply for a two- or three-year in-college scholarship available through the Professor of Military Science.

You may apply for a scholarship for your last two (or three) years of college even if you were not a member of an AROTC unit for your freshman or sophomore year. You should realize, however, that your chances of winning a scholarship are greater if you have been a cadet, since you will have had the opportunity to show your motivation for the Army, an important factor in the selection for in-college scholarships. If you are not an AROTC cadet when you win a two-year in-college scholarship, you will go to a special six-week Basic Camp in the summer where you will be taught the first two years of military science so you can join the Army ROTC Advanced Course as a junior. You may also attend the Basic Camp without a scholarship and try for one of the 300 scholarships awarded there.

If you are enrolled in a junior college, you may try for a two-year scholarship provided you are also accepted as a transfer student at an eligible four-year institution.

For in-college scholarships, the eligibility criteria, benefits, obligations, medical standards, career opportunities, and service obligations are the same as for the four-year scholarships. (See the previous pages for details.)

There are also two-year in-college scholarships for students who are majoring in nursing. Upon commissioning as a second lieutenant, these graduates join the Army Nurse Corps and are assigned to one of the Army's 48 medical centers in the United States and overseas.

For more information about two- and three-year Army ROTC scholarships, contact the Professor of Military Science at an Army ROTC unit near you.

NAVY ROTC

As a country that borders two oceans, the United States has had a need for a Navy to exercise control of the seas in time of war since its first days as a republic. From the 1700s to the present, going from sail to steam to nuclear power, the Navy has been a strong and effective arm of the U.S. Armed Forces. The Navy Department not only includes the submarines, surface ships, and aircraft of the Navy, it also embraces the Marine Corps. The Marines are the land-based extension of Naval sea power, and for over 200 years they have been considered an elite branch of the United States military establishment.

While the Army may have had a head start on the Navy in the founding of both a service academy (West Point in 1802, Annapolis in 1845) and ROTC (Army ROTC in 1919, Navy ROTC in 1926), the Navy was the first service to establish an ROTC scholarship program that commissioned Regular officers upon graduation from civilian colleges, thus placing them on an equal footing with their colleagues from the Naval Academy. The success of Navy ROTC scholarships, called the Holloway Plan after its founder, Admiral William Holloway, set the example for both the Army and the Air Force to initiate their own ROTC scholarship programs.

Since their earliest days, the Naval Academy and NROTC have been a commissioning program for both Navy ensigns and Marine Corps second lieutenants. In these two officer training programs, the role of the Marine Corps is similar to the relationship that exists within the Navy as a whole. The Marine Corps comes under the Naval organization but maintains its own distinctive identity. NROTC midshipmen who have selected the Marine option follow a Navy path for their first two years before switching over to specific Marine training at the start of their junior year. During the academic year future second lieutenants are taught courses dealing with the Marine Corps subjects and take their final summer training session at Quantico, Virginia.

The Navy has the fewest ROTC host colleges of the three services, numbering 64 in 1985–86. In addition there are 118 institutions that have cross-enrollment agreements, for a total of 182 colleges to choose from if you win the Navy ROTC scholarship. A list of these colleges is contained in Appendix C. Because of its relatively small size, Navy ROTC offers fewer scholarships and commissions only 1,600 Navy and Marine Corps officers each year, far fewer than the Army's 10,500 and the Air Force's 3,200. For 1985–86, there are 8,000 Navy ROTC scholarships. Of the 7,200 four-year scholarships in effect in a given year, 2,200 will be given to students entering college as freshmen. The remaining 800 awards are two- and three-year in-college scholarships used to fill vacancies that occur when four-year scholarship recipients withdraw.

Besides being the smallest of the three ROTC programs, the Navy has the toughest medical standards and places a somewhat heavier demand on a scholarship recipient while enrolled in college. A greater time commitment is called for in the Naval Science classes themselves, in the requirement to take other college courses, and also during the summer, with a Navy cruise scheduled each year. On the other hand, the Navy is less restrictive about your major than the Army or Air Force. The Navy does not have selection quotas based on academic field. Their approach is to permit you to choose from among a wide range of study areas but to make sure you have adequate technical preparation by requiring math and physics courses at the college level.

THE FOUR-YEAR SCHOLARSHIP FOR HIGH SCHOOL SENIORS

Scholarship Benefits

Winners of the four-year scholarship receive:

1. tuition and academic fees
2. books
3. $100 per month for the academic year
4. a travel allowance from your home to college to begin your freshman year
5. payment during summer training at a rate of $400 per month
6. uniforms
7. free flights on military passenger aircraft when there is space available.

Scholarship Obligations

In return for the scholarship you are required to:

1. study in an approved academic field and meet the college's requirements for a bachelor's degree
2. for Navy midshipmen: complete a one-semester course in a foreign language and one-year courses in both calculus and physics
   for Marine Corps students: complete one-semester courses in both military affairs and national security policy

3. enlist in the Naval or Marine Corps Reserve, enroll in the NROTC Unit, meet the Naval Science course requirements
4. attend three summer training periods, each four to six weeks long
5. upon graduation, accept a commission as an ensign in the Navy or a second lieutenant in the Marine Corps
6. serve a minimum of four years on active duty.

Application and Selection

ELIGIBILITY STANDARDS

To receive a four-year scholarship you must:

1. be a United States citizen
2. graduate from high school but not be enrolled in college
3. be at least 17 years old but no more than 21
4. be accepted by a college with an NROTC unit on campus or with a cross-enrollment agreement
5. plan to pursue an approved course of study
6. be of good moral character and have no personal convictions against serving in the military.

When you apply for a scholarship you will be asked to select either the Navy or Marine Corps option. You should do this based on your own personal sense of which service is best for you; the competition is equally strong for both programs. Marine Corps training is quite demanding in physical fitness and discipline. You should be quite certain that you are prepared for such a rigorous regimen before you choose the Marine Corps option. Once enrolled in an NROTC Unit, you may change your mind and switch from the Marine Corps to the Navy or from the Navy to the Marine Corps. Marine Corps students comprise about 1/6 of the total number of Navy midshipmen.

THE SELECTION PROCESS

To become a Navy finalist, you need to score at least 430 verbal and 520 math on the SAT, or score at least 18 in English and 24 in math on the ACT.

To become a Marine Corps finalist, you need to score 1000 (combined math and verbal) on the SAT, or score 45 (combined math and English) on the ACT.

High school class rank and grade point average are also considered, but there is no specified minimum.

If you are chosen as a finalist, you are next required to:

1. complete an application that includes your high school transcript, a report of your extracurricular activities, and teacher recommendations
2. report for an interview with a panel of Naval officers
3. take a medical exam.

INTENDED COURSE OF STUDY

Unlike the Army and Air Force, the Navy and Marine Corps do not have selection quotas based on academic field. You may major in virtually any subject except the health professions (such as medicine, dentistry and veterinary science).

MEDICAL REQUIREMENTS

Applicants must pass a medical exam to qualify for an NROTC scholarship. The standards below are not a complete list, but are intended to give you a general idea of the medical requirements.

1. *Height and Weight*

   Weight must be proportional to height. (See the chart in Appendix F.)

Height Range	Men:	Navy	5'2" to 6'6"
		Marines	5'6" to 6'6"
	Women:	Navy	5'0" to 6'6"
		Marines	5'0" to 6'6"

2. *Eyesight*

   Distant and near vision: 20/20 in each eye without correction. Up to one-third of the scholarship recipients may receive waivers if their vision is correctable to 20/20 provided refractive error does not exceed +/- 5.50 diopters. Color vision: Normal color vision is required for the Navy. There is no color vision requirement for the Marine Corps.

3. *Hearing*

   Allowable decibel loss varies from 30 in low frequencies to 60 at high frequencies.

4. *Allergies*

   No severe hay fever. No symptoms of asthma since age 12.

5. *Heart*

   Normal heartbeat. No hypertension or history of cardiovascular problems.

6. *Teeth*

   Must be in excellent dental health.

   Note: You should take care of any correctable deficiencies before you report for a physical.

SELECTION TIMETABLE

Early Selection

If you want to be a candidate for early selection, you should take the SAT or ACT in the spring of your junior year in high school, although it is possible that scores from the early fall test in your senior year may meet the deadline.

Early November	NROTC application deadline
December 15	Navy notifies winners subject to passing the medical exam

Regular Selection

November	Latest date to take SAT or ACT
Fall/Early winter	Apply to the colleges of your choice
Midwinter	Take the medical exam
Late January	NROTC application deadline
March 15	Navy notifies winners

Attending College

YOUR OBLIGATION TO THE NAVY UNIT

You will be required to take four years of Naval Science courses. Classes meet for three hours each week and the drill period takes an additional one and a half hours per week. In the freshman year, the courses are Introduction to Naval Science and Naval Engineering; for sophomore year, Naval Weapons and Seapower; for junior year, Navigation and Naval Operations; and for senior year, Leadership and Management. If you have chosen the Marine Corps option, you will be taught Evolution of Warfare and Amphibious Warfare in place of the Navy courses in your junior and senior years. During drills you will participate in training that extends beyond the Naval Science courses, especially military formations, physical conditioning, and practical exercises.

At a typical college, you will receive academic credit for nearly all your Naval Science courses, which total from 22 to 24 credit hours. Although NROTC classes may be more time-consuming than those offered by the Army and Air Force, it is somewhat less likely that you will have to take Naval Science courses in addition to your normal academic workload.

The NROTC Unit will also sponsor activities in addition to classes and drills. As a midshipman you will have the opportunity to participate in athletic and social functions or to be a member of a drill team.

YOUR ACADEMIC PROGRAM IN COLLEGE

NROTC midshipmen have to take one year of both calculus and physics, and one semester of a foreign language. Nonscience majors must devote one half of their electives to science, math or engineering courses. Marine option students are required to take a one-semester course in both military affairs and national security policy.

SUMMER TRAINING

You will have military duty each summer. As a Navy midshipman, during the summer prior to your sophomore year and again in the summer before your senior year, you will serve aboard a ship. During the other summer you will be introduced to amphibious warfare and flight training. Marine Corps option students join their Navy classmates for the first two summers before attending camp at Quantico, Virginia, prior to their senior year.

GRADUATE SCHOOL OPPORTUNITIES

Although the Navy or Marine Corps will sometimes permit a student to delay reporting to active duty to attend graduate school, the vast majority of new officers proceed directly to Navy duty stations or to the Marine Corps Basic School. Opportunities for graduate school will occur later in the career of a Naval or Marine Corps officer.

Active Duty Requirements

LENGTH OF SERVICE

The minimum obligation is four years for both the Navy and Marine Corps. If you choose submarine duty, you will be required to serve four years after approximately one and a half years of training. If you decide on either Navy or Marine Corps aviation, your minimum active duty is five years after flight training, which runs from one to one and a half years.

TYPES OF JOBS

Navy

After you are commissioned as an ensign, there are three branches of the Navy in which you can serve.

1. Surface Warfare. Here you will be assigned to sea duty on board a ship after a brief period of specialized training. Regardless of the type of ship—tanker, destroyer, or aircraft carrier—your duties will involve management, leadership, and knowledge of Naval operations.
2. Submarines. Before reporting to a submarine as a division officer, you will first undergo a rigorous graduate program in nuclear power and propulsion systems followed by specific training aboard a submarine. You will then proceed to the fleet.
3. Aviation. You may be either a flight officer or a pilot. In either case, you will be assigned to flight training for 12–18 months before reporting to a fleet squadron. Naval flight officers serve as crew members and are in charge of navigation and weapons systems. Naval pilots fly a variety of aircraft, many of which operate from aircraft carriers.

Marine Corps

After you are commissioned as a second lieutenant, you will attend the Basic School at Quantico, Virginia, for 21 weeks of further training. In Basic School you will continue your Marine Corps professional education, particularly in areas like marksmanship, infantry tactics, and amphibious operations. From the knowledge and training you gain in Basic School, you will select one of the Marine Corps specialties: Infantry, Tracked Vehicles, Aviation (Marine Corps pilots go through Naval flight training), Field Artillery, Engineering, Communications, Supply or Computer Science. Unless you are selected to go to flight training, you will proceed to the Fleet Marine Force after Basic School.

For more information about the four-year Naval ROTC scholarship, see your high school guidance counselor, check with a Naval ROTC unit on a college campus, or contact:

Commander, Navy Recruiting Command (Code 314)
4015 Wilson Boulevard
Arlington, Virginia 22203

TWO- AND THREE-YEAR SCHOLARSHIPS FOR COLLEGE STUDENTS

As with the Army and Air Force, you may enroll in an NROTC unit as a non-scholarship student and take the same Navy courses as a scholarship recipient. If you then wish to apply for a scholarship for the remaining 2 or 3 years of your undergraduate education, you request a nomination from the Professor of Naval Science and enter the competition for an in-college scholarship.

It is also possible to receive a 2-year Navy scholarship even if you are not a member of an NROTC unit. If you are interested, you should contact the Professor of Naval Science in the fall of your sophomore year. If you are selected, you attend the Naval Science Institute during the summer and then join the NROTC unit for your junior and senior years. You should bear in mind, however, that your chances of receiving a scholarship are better if you are already a member of an NROTC unit, since you will have a military "track record" that is helpful in the selection process.

For in-college scholarships, the eligibility criteria, benefits, obligations, medical standards, career opportunities, and service obligation are the same as the four-year scholarships. (See the previous pages for details.)

To find out more about 2- and 3-year scholarships, check with a Naval ROTC unit near you.

AIR FORCE ROTC

The Air Force is the youngest of the military services. In the early 1900s, as military airpower began to grow, the Army created a special division called the Army Air Corps. At the conclusion of World War II, Congress decided that the use of aircraft in warfare had become so important that the United States needed a military branch specializing in air power. As a result, Congress passed a law in 1947 that created the United States Air Force as a separate service.

Air Force ROTC was established as well in 1947 and it has continued to commission officers for 38 years. In 1955, the Air Force Academy was founded, providing another way for the Air Force to commission second lieutenants directly upon their graduation from college.

The Air Force has the same mixture of scholarship programs for college students as the other services—the four-year national scholarship competition for high school students, various in-college scholarships for undergraduates, and enrollment in the Air Force Academy. There are, however, distinctive characteristics of the Air Force's programs that are important for you to consider as you think about which service is right for you.

Within the Air Force as a whole, the Air Force Academy is virtually the only source of Regular officers as well as the primary producer of pilots and navigators. So if you are fairly sure you want to be a career Air Force officer or you want to enter flight training, you should first try for the Air Force Academy. The Air Force ROTC program, by contrast, has a separate role: to supply Reserve officers who will serve on active duty as scientists or engineers in areas that support Air Force flight operations. There is a clear distinction between the role of Academy graduates and that of ROTC graduates. While there are some exceptions, the general rule is that the Air Force Academy produces Regular officers who will be assigned to flight duties while the AFROTC produces Reserve officers who will provide scientific, engineering, and management support.

This arrangement is quite different from the Navy (and the Army to some extent) where both academy and ROTC graduates are commissioned as Regular officers and are assigned to the same kinds of active duty jobs. The more limited role that is designed for an Air Force second lieutenant who graduates from ROTC will appeal to some people for various reasons. For example, the physical standards are more lenient for AFROTC than for the other scholarship programs. Also, it is likely that your active duty assignment will be closely related to your academic field. If, for example, you major in aeronautical engineering, you probably will work with avionics systems rather than in personnel or supply.

There are 151 colleges that host Air Force ROTC units and another 658 institutions that have cross-enrollment agreements. A list of these colleges is contained in Appendix D. A cross-enrollment arrangement means you can attend a college near one that has an AFROTC unit on campus and commute to take the ROTC courses. A student attending any one of the four-year colleges among the 809 may hold an Air Force scholarship—either the four-year award for high school seniors or an in-college scholarship for students already enrolled. If you are attending a two-year college, you need to be accepted as a transfer student by a four-year college in order to qualify for the scholarship.

For 1985–86, there are 8,000 AFROTC scholarships of which approximately 2,000 will be four-year scholarships given to students entering college as freshmen, with a total of approximately 6,500 students holding four-year scholarships in any given year. The other 1,500 are used as in-college scholarships for either two or three years.

THE FOUR-YEAR SCHOLARSHIP FOR HIGH SCHOOL SENIORS

Scholarship Benefits

Winners of four-year scholarships receive:

1. Tuition and fees

2. an allowance for books
3. $100 per month during the academic year
4. a travel allowance from your home to college to begin your freshman year
5. payment for summer field training at a rate of approximately $400 per month
6. uniforms
7. free flights on military passenger aircraft when there is space available.

Scholarship Obligations

In return for the scholarship you are required to:

1. study in the academic area in which the scholarship is offered and meet the college's requirements for a bachelor's degree
2. enlist in the Air Force Reserve, enroll in an AFROTC unit, and complete the four-year Aerospace Studies program
3. complete one semester of a foreign language
4. attend one four-week summer training period
5. upon graduation, accept a commission as an Air Force Reserve second lieutenant
6. serve at least four years on active duty.

Application and Selection

ELIGIBILITY STANDARDS

To receive a four-year scholarship you must:

1. be a United States citizen
2. graduate from high school but not be enrolled in college
3. be at least 17 years old but no more than 21
4. be accepted by a college with an AFROTC unit on campus or one with a cross-enrollment agreement
5. plan to pursue a specific course of study
6. be of good moral character and have no personal convictions against serving in the military.

THE SELECTION PROCESS

To become a finalist you need to:

1. have a high school grade point average of 2.5 out of 4.0
2. be in the top 25% of your high school class
3. score at least 1000 on the SAT (minimum 500 math, 450 verbal) or 23 on the ACT (minimum 20 math, 19 English).

If you are chosen as a finalist, you are required to:

1. complete an application which includes your high school transcript, a report of your extracurricular activities, and teacher recommendations
2. have a personal interview with a panel of Air Force officers
3. take a medical exam.

INTENDED COURSE OF STUDY IN COLLEGE

Your chances of winning a four-year scholarship vary greatly depending on the subject you plan to major in. The Air Force allocates ROTC scholarships to fill its need for officers with certain skills. Although the Air Force requirements vary somewhat from year to year, there is a strong emphasis on engineering majors, with some openings for scientists. Very few scholarships are given to students studying liberal arts. For 1985–86, the scholarships were divided as follows:

Engineers	80%
Science majors (architecture, computer science, math, meteorology, and physics)	17%
Nontechnical majors (accounting, business, economics, history, and management)	3%

Unless you are fairly certain you want to major in engineering or science, the AFROTC is probably not the program for you, as the Army and Navy have considerably more openings for liberal arts majors.

MEDICAL REQUIREMENTS

If you become a finalist, you must pass a comprehensive medical exam. The standards shown below are not a complete list, but are intended to give you a general idea of the medical requirements.

1. *Height and Weight*
   Weight must be proportional to height. (See the chart in Appendix F.)

Height Range	Men	5'0" to 6'8"
	Women	5'0" to 6'8"

2. *Eyesight*
   Correctable distant and near vision can be somewhat worse than 20/20, averaging about 20/40 in each eye. There are no standards for color vision.
3. *Hearing*
   Allowable decibel loss varies from 25 in low frequencies to 90 at high frequencies.
4. *Allergies*
   No severe hay fever. No symptoms of asthma since age 12.
5. *Heart*
   Normal heartbeat. No hypertension or history of cardiovascular problems.
6. *Teeth*
   Numerous unfilled cavities may be a cause for disqualification.

Note: You should take care of any correctable deficiencies before you report for a physical.

SELECTION TIMETABLE

The Air Force chooses scholarship winners on a "rolling" basis with selection boards meeting in November, January, and March. The earlier you apply, the greater your chance of acceptance.

You must meet these deadlines:

December	Latest date to take SAT or ACT
December 1	ROTC application deadline
Fall/Early winter	Apply to the colleges of your choice
Late fall/winter	Take the medical exam
December, February, and April	Air Force notifies winners

Keep in mind you must be admitted both to an Air Force host college and into the academic major you specified on your ROTC application. For example, if the Air Force approves your scholarship for study in engineering, your college must accept you into its engineering school.

Attending College

YOUR OBLIGATION TO THE AIR FORCE UNIT

You will be required to take four years of AFROTC courses, called Aerospace Studies. During your first two years in college you take the General Military Course for two and a half hours per week—one hour of class and one and a half hours of drill. The General Military Course covers an introduction to the military and the development of U.S. air power. In the junior and senior years, the time commitment increases to four and a half hours per week—three hours of class in the Professional Officer's Course and one and a half hours of drill. In the Professional Officer's Course you learn about management skills and American defense policy. During the drill periods you will participate in military formations, physical fitness training, and leadership exercises.

Depending on the terms of the agreement between the ROTC Unit and the college, you may receive academic credit for your AFROTC courses. At a typical college, about 75% of the Aerospace Studies courses count towards your graduation requirement. If an AFROTC course is not approved for credit, you will have to take the course in addition to your normal academic workload.

Besides AFROTC classes and drills, you will have the opportunity to participate in voluntary activities sponsored by the unit. These usually include a drill team, social events, and trips to Air Force bases.

Keep in mind that if you are interested in flying, as either a pilot or navigator, the AFROTC scholarship program is probably not the path you should be taking. If you realize this after you've enrolled in AFROTC, you may be able to qualify for navigator school and have your scholarship shifted to that duty assignment. However, if you are selected for pilot training, there is a good chance that you will lose the last two years of your scholarship since the Air Force has a surplus of pilot candidates and therefore does not normally pay tuition costs for such students.

YOUR ACADEMIC PROGRAM IN COLLEGE

Besides taking specific AFROTC courses, you must make satisfactory progress in the major subject the Air Force has approved, and complete a semester of a foreign language. The Air Force is firm about requiring you to stay with the academic field you specified when you were selected. If you switch your major to a subject that is in a different academic area (for example, from engineering to science, or from science to liberal arts) you will lose your scholarship but you will be given the chance to compete for a scholarship in the new field. If you are successful, you will regain your financial aid. You should realize, however, that the competition is very tough if you try to move from engineering to either science or liberal arts.

SUMMER TRAINING

You will be required to attend one four-week field training camp at an Air Force base during the summer, normally between your sophomore and junior years. This is your opportunity to learn firsthand what the Air Force is really like and to think seriously about the type of active duty assignment you would like upon graduation.

GRADUATE SCHOOL OPPORTUNITIES

You may request a delay in reporting to active duty to attend graduate school at your own expense. You may also apply to a program in which the Air Force pays for your graduate school while you serve on active duty. The Air Force offers a number of such opportunities in areas ranging from health professions to meteorology. The largest is the Minuteman Education Program—a special program for missile launch officers that can lead to a graduate degree in business or management.

If you don't go on to graduate school directly after college, and you decide to stay in the Air Force after your first tour of duty, in all likelihood you will have the opportunity to continue your education at a later time. The Air Force places a strong emphasis on graduate study, and 60–70% of its officers eventually obtain advanced degrees.

Active Duty Requirements

LENGTH OF SERVICE

If you are not involved in flying, you must serve a minimum of four years on active duty. Navigators have a five-year obligation after a training period of approximately six months. Pilots serve six years after about a year of flight training. If the Air Force pays for your graduate education, your active duty will be extended in proportion to the time it takes you to get an advanced degree. There are exceptions to this rule, however. For example, the Minuteman Education Program is designed to enable you to obtain an advanced degree within your normal service obligation.

TYPES OF JOBS

Upon graduation you will be commissioned as a second lieutenant in the United States Air Force Reserve and ordered to active duty. The duty assignment you will receive is highly dependent on the technical skills you acquired while you were in college and your overall academic and military record. Flight personnel and missile officers come from a variety of academic backgrounds, but, as with most Air Force jobs, a good background in math and science is important. Beyond these two assignment areas, there is a fairly close relationship between your academic major and the type of active duty you can expect. Here are some examples:

College Major	Air Force Duty
Administration/Management	Accounting and Finance, Personnel, Supply, Computer Systems, Food Services, Space Systems
Arts, Humanities, and Education	Air Intelligence, Education and Training, Public Affairs
Computer Science	Computer Systems, Computer Operations
Engineering	Space Systems Analyst, Aircraft and Missile Maintenance, Project Engineer, Research, Management Analysis, Manufacturing Engineer
Law	Judge Advocate
Medical Science	Physician, Dentist, Pharmacist, Therapist, Nurse
Science	Space Systems, Communications, Weather, Research, Computer Systems, Scientific Analyst, Air Intelligence
Social Studies	Air Intelligence, Education and Training, Management, History, Executive Support

For more information about four-year Air Force ROTC scholarships, see your high school guidance counselor, check with an AFROTC unit on a college campus, or talk to an Air Force Regional Admissions Counselor. You can find out the location of an Air Force counselor near you by calling 205-293-2091. Or you can contact:

AFROTC
Maxwell Air Force Base
Alabama 36112
Telephone: 205-293-2091

TWO- AND THREE-YEAR SCHOLARSHIPS FOR COLLEGE STUDENTS

Nationwide, there are about 800 new AFROTC scholarships awarded each year to college students, either to cadets who were not previously on scholarship or to undergraduates who have not yet joined a unit. Both two- and three-year scholarships are available for students who have sufficient time remaining in their academic programs (including graduate work) to meet the scholarship requirements. For example, if you apply for a three-year scholarship as a sophomore, you would have to be enrolled in a five-year academic program, such as engineering or architecture. Like the four-year scholarship for high school students, most of the in-college scholarships are awarded to science or engineering majors. There are, however, two-year scholarships available for students in nontechnical fields as well as for navigators and missile officers.

Although in-college scholarships are open to all students, your chances of selection are improved if you are a member of an AFROTC Unit. In actual practice, virtually all the three-year scholarships go to AFROTC cadets. Therefore, if you do not sign up as a freshman, the two-year scholarship is normally the only one for which you will be able to compete. Furthermore, if you are already a cadet you have the opportunity to show your motivation for the military service, an important plus in the selection process. A student who wins a scholarship but who is not already a member of an AFROTC Unit will be required to take the equivalent of the first two years of Aerospace Studies at a special summer session. If you are a junior college student you have to be accepted at a four-year institution before you can receive a two- or three-year scholarship.

The eligibility criteria, benefits, obligations, medical standards, active duty opportunities and service obligation for AFROTC in-college scholarships are the same as for the four-year scholarship for high school seniors. (See the previous pages for details.)

The Air Force has special in-college scholarships for students majoring in the health professions. There are two- and three-year AFROTC scholarships for undergraduates who are pursuing a premedical degree. After graduation, recipients of these scholarships attend medical school while serving on active duty. Two-year scholarships also are available to students who are majoring in nursing. Upon graduation, Air Force ROTC nurses enter an internship program as their first duty assignment.

If you are interested in more information about an in-college scholarship, check with a college AFROTC unit near you.

SUMMARY AND COMPARISON OF ROTC SCHOLARSHIP PROGRAMS

The following table summarizes the important aspects of the ROTC scholarship programs.

	Army	Navy/ Marine Corps	Air Force
Eligibility Standards	**4 year scholarships:** U.S. citizen, high school graduate, age 17–21, plan to pursue approved course of study, of good moral character, no personal convictions against serving in the military **2 and 3 year scholarships:** all of the above plus enrolled in college, maintaining satisfactory progress toward degree		
Medical Requirements **Eyesight** Normal vision	correctable to 20/20	20/20 except 1/3 on waivers	correctable to approximately 20/40
Color vision	distinguish between vivid red and vivid green	Navy: normal color vision Marines: no color vision requirement	no color vision requirement
Height Men	5'0" to 6'8"	Navy: 5'2" to 6'6" Marines: 5'6" to 6'6"	5'0" to 6'8"
Women	4'10" to 6'0"	5'0" to 6'6"	5'0" to 6'8"
Scholarship Benefits	tuition, books, $100 per month, travel allowance, pay for summer training, free flights on military aircraft when space permits		

(continued on next page)

Summary and Comparison of ROTC Scholarship Programs (continued)

	Army	Navy/ Marine Corps	Air Force
Military Requirements	Enlist in the Reserve, complete the ROTC military science program, may hold scholarship for one year before obligation begins. **2 and 3 year scholarships:** obligation commences upon enrolling in military science course.		
Academic Requirements	Take one semester of a foreign language, meet the college's requirements for a bachelor's degree.		
	study in a specified academic field	Navy: take one year of calculus and one year of physics Marines: take one semester of military affairs and one semester of national security policy	study in a specified academic field
Summer Training	1 summer	3 summers	1 summer
	2 and 3 year scholarships: usually 1 or 2 summers depending on previous ROTC affiliation		
Type of Commission	Regular or Reserve 2nd lieutenant	Regular Navy Ensign or Marine 2nd lieutenant	Reserve 2nd lieutenant (small number commissioned as Regulars)
Length of Active Duty	unless assigned to the Reserve Force, minimum of 4 years	minimum of 4 years	minimum of 4 years
Where You Can Enroll	314 host colleges **2 and 3 year scholarships:** 1,454 cross-enrollment or extension centers	182 host or cross-enrollment colleges	809 host or cross-enrollment colleges

Summary and Comparison of ROTC Scholarship Programs (continued)

	Army	Navy/ Marine Corps	Air Force
Academic Quotas	30% engineering 25% physical science 20% business 10% social science 7% nursing 8% other	none	80% engineers 17% science 3% other

2 and 3 year scholarships: Army and Air Force quotas may be somewhat different depending on needs of the service

	Army	Navy/ Marine Corps	Air Force
Selection Calendar			
Early Plan	SAT/ACT in June Apply in Aug. Notification in Nov.	SAT/ACT in June or Oct. Apply in Nov. Notification in Dec.	none
Regular Plan	SAT/ACT no later than Dec. Apply by Dec. Notification in Mar.	SAT/ACT no later than Nov. Apply in Jan. Notification in Mar.	SAT/ACT no later than Dec. Apply by Dec. Notification in Dec., Feb., and Apr.

2 and 3 year scholarships: Application due fall or early spring of freshman or sophomore year at ROTC unit. Decisions made in late spring or summer

WHERE ROTC UNITS ARE LOCATED

You should refer to the appendixes to see if the colleges you are currently interested in offer ROTC. Appendix A lists all colleges in alphabetical order that have any kind of ROTC unit. Appendixes B, C, and D list colleges with ROTC units by military service.

Chapter 3

The Service Academies

Next to ROTC, the most common way to combine college with military officer training is by attending a service academy. The Army, Navy, Air Force, Coast Guard, and Merchant Marine each has its own academy. Marine Corps officers are trained at the Naval Academy. These academies offer a high-quality technically oriented education (equal to any of the top engineering schools in the country) with all your college expenses paid by the federal government. In other words, your education will be free.

If you go to college at a service academy you will be a full-time member of the military and, except for vacation periods, you will wear a uniform and be subject to military rules and regulations, the most important being a regimented lifestyle and a strict discipline code. The financial rewards are, however, proportionately greater in return for this more extensive military involvement.

Before you decide to apply to a service academy, you should have a strong feeling that the military is an occupation that appeals to you. You should not apply merely because an academy offers a free education or because someone else thinks it is the place for you. You should be fairly settled on the idea of a career as a military officer. This does not mean you have to be 100% certain; that is too much to expect of a 17 or 18 year old who is only beginning to think seriously about future plans. On the other hand, your career goals should be at least roughly defined and you should be able to picture yourself serving as an officer for a number of years.

Life at a military academy is a very rigorous and special type of education. Your academic interests should be in pursuing a bachelor of science rather than a liberal arts degree. On the personal side, you should be the type of person who is willing to become completely involved in military life as a college student. You will attend an academy for four years, with only short periods off for vacations. College life will consist of a well-structured daily schedule, a heavy academic workload, adherence to an honor code and considerable physical activity.

The nature of cadet or midshipman life at a service academy can be illustrated by describing a typical yearly calendar as well as the daily routine.

Yearly Calendar

	From	*To*
Freshman Summer Indoctrination	1 July	15 August
Fall Semester	16 August	22 December
Christmas Vacation	23 December	8 January
Winter Semester	9 January	10 March
Spring Vacation	11 March	17 March
Spring Semester	18 March	16 May
Summer Vacation	17 May	17 June
Summer Camp/Cruise	18 June	15 August

In other words, as a cadet or midshipman at a service academy, out of a 52-week year you will attend class 36 weeks, have summer training for 8 weeks, and be on vacation for 8 weeks.

Daily Routine

6:00 a.m.	Wake up
6:45 a.m.–7:15 a.m.	Breakfast
7:15 a.m.–7:30 a.m.	Morning Formation
7:30 a.m.–12:00 noon	Morning Classes
12:00 noon–1:00 p.m.	Lunch
1:00 p.m.–3:30 p.m.	Afternoon Classes
3:30 p.m.–6:00 p.m.	Military Drill, Athletics, Extracurricular Activities
6:00 p.m.–7:00 p.m.	Dinner
7:00 p.m.–11:00 p.m.	Study
11:00 p.m.	Lights out

Usually this schedule goes on for five and one half days each week, from Monday morning to Saturday noon. Upperclassmen normally have liberty from Saturday noon until Sunday night. Time off for freshmen is quite restricted, with only an occasional opportunity to leave the academy grounds. The amount of liberty and other privileges vary with senority (the higher your class, the more free time you get), responsibility, and performance.

Although the number of officers produced each year by the service academies is less than the number that come through the ROTC programs, the academies are a very important source of officers, particularly among those who intend to make the military their career. The following table summarizes the size of the different academies.

	West Point	Annapolis	Air Force	Coast Guard	Merchant Marine
Number of Cadets or Midshipmen	4,500	4,500	4,500	850	1,000
Number of Officers Produced Each Year	1,000	1,000	950	150	250

THE ADMISSIONS PROCESS AT WEST POINT, ANNAPOLIS, AND THE AIR FORCE ACADEMY

Because of the similarities among West Point, Annapolis, and the Air Force Academy in the process by which they offer appointments (the military term for admission), the descriptions for all three are given together below. Because the Coast Guard Academy and Merchant Marine Academy follow a somewhat different admissions procedure, their guidelines are given separately in the sections devoted to them.

Eligibility Standards

You need to be a U.S. citizen, unmarried (and single while you are enrolled at an academy), of good moral character, and at least 17 but no more than 22 years old in the year of admission.

Precandidate Questionnaire

First, you will fill out a brief, two-page questionnaire that registers you as an applicant. If you meet the basic eligibility standards, the academy will send you a package of admissions material including information about how to ask for a nomination.

Requesting a Nomination

The next step is to be nominated by an official source, normally your Congressman. Each Congressman has a set number of nominees he or she can recommend for admission. The military service itself may also nominate candidates who are sons and daughters of past and present members of the Armed Forces. The process of obtaining a nomination is not as complicated as it appears: You simply write a standard letter to the Representative from your district and to your Senators. You do not have to have political influence nor is it necessary that you know your Congressman. The nomination procedure is merely an additional screening that takes place within your state or Congressional district.

Getting Admitted

If you receive a nomination, you go through the next phase of the admissions process which involves evaluation of your SAT or ACT scores, a review of your high school record, including teachers' recommendations, a physical fitness test, and a medical exam. The academy admissions office offers appointments to the most qualified from among those who have met all the standards. They look carefully at a combination of factors, weighing academic performance, high school activities, and strength of character. West Point, Annapolis, and the Air Force Academy all have "rolling" admissions plans. Since they accept students as applications become complete, it is to your advantage to apply early.

Chapter 1 contains information about the kinds of high school courses you should take if you are seriously considering a service academy. It also describes the typical profile of a successful applicant. You may wish to reread that section.

COSTS

At the four military academies—West Point, Annapolis, Air Force Academy and Coast Guard Academy—the cost of tuition, room and board is paid by the federal government. Cadets also receive $500 per month from which the academy deducts the cost of uniforms, books, and laundry. During your freshman year you will have approximately $60 remaining each month to cover personal expenses. From your sophomore year on you will have more spending money available since most of your uniform costs are charged in your first year. There is also a travel allowance based on the distance from your home to the academy. Although it offers a nearly free education, the Merchant Marine Academy has a somewhat different arrangement; see page 52.

THE UNITED STATES MILITARY ACADEMY

Located in West Point, New York, the U.S. Military Academy prepares young men and women for careers as Army officers. West Point is quite selective in its admissions. Each year approximately 13,000 students apply and 6,200 receive nominations. Of these, 2,700 are judged to be fully qualified scholastically, medically, and physically. About 1,900 are eventually admitted and about 1,400 accept admission into the freshman class.

Here is a summary of things you should know about West Point.

Admissions Calendar

Spring of junior year in high school (preferred) or early senior year	Fill out precandidate questionnaire
Spring of junior year (preferred) or early senior year	Request a nomination

Early Selection

No later than November	Take SAT or ACT
By December 1	Apply

Regular Selection

No later than February	Take SAT or ACT
By March 21	Apply
During the West Point admissions processing period	Take medical exam and physical fitness test
November to April	The Army notifies those who receive appointments

Medical Requirements

The standards are the same as for the Army ROTC scholarship; see page 16.

Physical Fitness Requirements

To be offered an appointment you have to pass the West Point physical aptitude exam. This test consists of a shuttle run, kneeling basketball throw, standing long jump, and pull-ups (for men) or flexed arm hang (for women).

Graduation Requirements

You will be expected to:

1. attend West Point for four years—fall and spring semesters and a summer session each year
2. major in one of these four fields of study: Applied Sciences and Engineering, Basic Sciences, Humanities, or National Security and Public Affairs
3. maintain a 2.0 GPA (C average)
4. successfully pass all required courses and physical and military training; show satisfactory conduct, including adherence to an honor code
5. graduate with a Bachelor of Science degree, accept a Regular Army commission as a second lieutenant.

Active Duty Requirements

Service Obligation

The minimum service requirement is five years. This time commitment will be extended if you attend graduate school at the Army's expense. Your service obligation may also increase if you attend certain Army branch schools, including flight training.

Types of Duty

Most newly commissioned second lieutenants report to their Army duty stations soon after graduation although a number of outstanding students win scholarships or fellowships for graduate study. Even if you don't go to graduate school directly from West Point, there will be many opportunities to pursue an advanced degree later in your career.

A West Point graduate will enter one of the branches of the Army listed in the Army ROTC section on page 19 and be expected to exercise important leadership and management responsibilities as a second lieutenant. By law, at least 80% of the cadets must be commissioned in a combat unit.

For more information about West Point, see your high school guidance counselor or contact:

Director of Admissions
U.S. Military Academy
West Point, New York 10996

Telephone: 914-938-4041

Your high school guidance counselor should also be able to put you in touch with the West Point field representative in your area.

THE UNITED STATES NAVAL ACADEMY

The U.S. Naval Academy is located in Annapolis, Maryland, on the shore of the Chesapeake Bay, about equal distance from Baltimore and Washington, D.C. Annapolis is looking for young men and women who are very motivated for either the Navy or Marine Corps.

Since Annapolis attracts a large number of well-qualified applicants, it is selective in its admissions. In a typical year there are about 14,000 applications. Of these, 6,600 receive nominations and 2,200 are judged to meet the Academy's scholastic, physical fitness, and medical standards. About 1,700 are admitted and 1,350 decide to attend.

Admissions Calendar

Spring of junior year in high school (preferred) or early senior year	Fill out a precandidate questionnaire
Spring of junior year (preferred) or early senior year	Request a nomination
No later than February	Take SAT or ACT Complete Naval Academy application

| During the Annapolis admissions processing period | Take medical exam and physical fitness test |
| October to April | The Navy notifies those who receive appointments |

Medical Requirements

The standards are the same as for the four-year NROTC scholarship, as described on page 24.

Physical Fitness Requirements

You must pass a physical fitness test consisting of pull-ups (for men) or flexed arm hang (for women), standing broad jump, kneeling basketball throw, and 300-yard shuttle run.

Graduation Requirements

You will be expected to:

1. attend Annapolis for four years—fall and spring semesters and a summer session each year
2. enroll in engineering, science or math unless you are one of the 20% approved to major in the humanities or social sciences
3. maintain a 2.0 GPA (C average)
4. successfully pass all required courses and physical and military training; show satisfactory conduct, including adherence to an honor code
5. graduate with a Bachelor of Science degree, accept a commission as an ensign in the Regular Navy or a second lieutenant in the Regular Marine Corps.

Active Duty Requirements

Service Obligation

Your active duty obligation is a minimum of five years. Should you choose submarines or aviation, your length of service will be extended by the twelve to eighteen months it takes to go through training.

Types of Duty

Since both Annapolis and NROTC graduates are commissioned as Regular officers in the Navy or Marine Corps, you will be assigned to the types of jobs that are listed on page 26 in the NROTC section of this chapter. As with the policy for ensigns and second lieutenants who come through NROTC, there are only a few opportunities for graduate study right after college, and those are primarily for outstanding students who have been successful in a fellowship competition. Even if you don't go to graduate school directly from Annapolis, there will be many opportunities to pursue an advanced degree later in your career.

For more information about Annapolis, see your high school guidance counselor or contact:

Director of Candidate Guidance
U.S. Naval Academy
Annapolis, Maryland 21402

Telephone: 301-267-4361

Your guidance counselor should also be able to give you the name of the Naval Academy Information Officer in your area.

THE UNITED STATES AIR FORCE ACADEMY

Located in Colorado Springs, Colorado, the U.S. Air Force Academy is the source of nearly all Regular Air Force officers, 75% of whom enter flight training as either pilots or navigators. To consider applying to the Air Force Academy you should be seriously interested in a career in the Air Force, most likely as a pilot or navigator.

The Air Force Academy is highly selective. In a typical year its admissions office receives 13,000 applications. Of these, 6,400 are nominated, 3,500 meet the academic, physical and medical standards, and 1,850 are admitted. On average, 1,450 of the admitted candidates decide to enroll.

Admissions Calendar

Spring of junior year in high school (preferred) or early senior year	Fill out precandidate questionnaire
Spring of junior year (preferred) or early senior year	Request a nomination
No later than the end of November	Take SAT or ACT
November	Apply for early selection
By end of January	Apply for regular selection
During the Academy processing period	Take medical exam and physical fitness test
November to April	The Air Force notifies those who receive appointments

Medical Requirements

Air Force Academy nonflying personnel have the same medical standards as Air Force ROTC scholarship recipients (see page 30). Those who plan to enter flight training must meet the eyesight requirements and height restrictions shown below.

Pilot: Uncorrected 20/20 vision. Normal color vision. Height 5'4" to 6'4".

Navigator: Distant vision: correctable to 20/20 but no worse than 20/70 uncorrected. Near vision: 20/20 uncorrected, normal color vision. Height 5'4" to 6'4".

Physical Fitness Requirements

You must pass a physical fitness test consisting of push-ups, sit-ups, pull-ups, and a 300-yard shuttle run.

Graduation Requirements

You will be expected to:

1. attend the Air Force Academy for four years—fall and spring semesters and a summer term each year
2. major in any one of 23 subject areas, including science, engineering, social science, and humanities
3. maintain a 2.0 GPA (C average)
4. successfully pass all required courses and physical and military training; show satisfactory conduct, including adherence to an honor code
5. graduate with a Bachelor of Science degree, accept a Regular Air Force commission as a second lieutenant.

Active Duty Requirements

Service Obligation

For nonflying officers, the minimum service obligation is 5 years. Navigators serve 5 years after about 6 months of training. Pilots are required to sign up for 6 years after approximately 1 year of flight training.

Types of Duty

Most newly commissioned second lieutenants go directly on active duty although a number of outstanding students win scholarships or fellowships for graduate study. Even if you don't proceed to graduate school right away, there will be many opportunities to pursue an advanced degree later in your Air Force career.

If you are not involved in aviation, you will be assigned to the types of active duty jobs described on page 33 in the AFROTC section.

If you are one of the 75% earmarked for flight training, you will end up as an aviator in either the Tactical Air Command (fighter aircraft), the Strategic Air Command (bombers), or a support group like the Military Airlift Command (transport planes).

For more information, see your high school guidance counselor or contact:

Cadet Admissions Office
USAF Academy
Colorado Springs, Colorado 80840

Telephone: 303-472-2640

Your high school guidance counselor should also be able to give the name of the Air Force Liaison Officer in your area.

THE COAST GUARD ACADEMY

The Coast Guard is one of the oldest military services, founded in 1790 when President George Washington asked Congress for a number of ships to guard the shores of the young republic. The United States Navy was formed eight years later in 1798 as the "sea-going" military force, but the need for a special service to patrol U.S. coastal waters remained and, in one form or another, has continued to the present day. During peacetime, the Coast Guard comes under the Department of Transportation and carries out eight primary duties: (1) encouraging boat safety; (2) conducting search and rescue missions; (3) maintaining aids to navigation; (4) regulating the Merchant Marine; (5) dealing with marine environmental protection; (6) enforcing maritime law; (7) ensuring port safety; and (8) conducting ice patrols.

When the United States is engaged in war, the Coast Guard becomes part of the Navy. In that role the Coast Guard may be called to serve anywhere in the world. For example, during World War II, Coast Guard cutters operated out of Greenland to help convoy American ships, and in the Vietnam War the Coast Guard was used in Southeast Asia to prevent the movement of enemy shipping.

The Coast Guard does not sponsor an ROTC program so the only way you can go through officer training while in college is by attending the U.S. Coast Guard Academy.

The Academy, founded in 1876, is located in New London, Connecticut, on the banks of the Thames River, not far from where it flows into Long Island Sound. Like West Point, Annapolis, and the Air Force Academy, the Coast Guard Academy is highly selective in admissions and is looking for top-notch students who have strong personal qualities and are interested in serving their country as military officers. The most distinctive aspect of the Coast Guard Academy's admission process is that it works like that of any other competitive college. Applicants submit the required material directly to the Coast Guard Academy admissions office and the most qualified are offered admission. Unlike the other four academies, an applicant does not have to be nominated by a Congressman. The absence of this requirement makes the Coast Guard Academy's admission process more straightforward and easier to deal with.

During a recent year, 6,900 students applied, and 520 were admitted. Of the admitted students, 250 actually enrolled. The Coast Guard Academy is considerably smaller than West Point, Annapolis, or the Air Force Academy (and about the same size as the Merchant Marine Academy), with 850 cadets compared to 4,500 for each of the other three.

The biggest difference between the Coast Guard and the other military services lies not so much in the nature of the Academy, but rather in the mission of the Coast Guard itself. As part of the Department of Defense, the purpose of the Army, Navy, Air Force and Marine Corps is to defend the United States against foreign aggression. In contrast, the Coast Guard, under the Department of Transportation, spends much of its time in a nonmilitary role—making waterways safer for boating, easier to navigate, and freer of accidents, oil spills, and other dangers. If this part of the Coast Guard's work—saving lives and protecting property—appeals to you, the Coast Guard Academy bears a close look.

Although the type of work you will do in the Coast Guard after you become an officer may be quite different from the jobs you would hold in the other services, student life at the Academies is similar. (See the yearly schedule and daily routine in the front of this chapter.) In your studies, you will concentrate on science or engineering with some courses in other areas. Outside of the classroom, you will be completely immersed in a military lifestyle, with a well-structured daily schedule, adherence to a discipline and honor code, and considerable physical activity. You will either attend classes or be involved in summer cruises for all but about two months of the year.

What follows is a summary of important points about the Coast Guard Academy.

High School Academic Preparation

The Coast Guard Academy has a minimum course requirement of three years of math and three years of English. In addition, a fourth year of both math and English is recommended along with courses in American history, a laboratory science, and a foreign language.

Eligibility Standards

You must be a United States citizen, unmarried (and single while enrolled at the Academy), of good moral character, and between 17 and 22 years old in the year of admission.

Getting Admitted

After you complete the admission application your credentials will be evaluated based on your high school grades, scores on either the SAT or ACT, teachers' recommendations, leadership potential as demonstrated by extracurricular activities, sports and community involvement, and your interest in becoming a Coast

Guard officer. The strength of a candidate's academic credentials is the most important single factor but the Academy also looks for a balance between grades and personal attributes.

The profile of a typical Coast Guard Academy cadet is similar to that of a student at the other academies. (See page 7.)

Admissions Calendar

June to December	Submit application
September through December	Take SAT or ACT
By January 15	All application material due
During the Coast Guard Academy admissions processing period	Take medical exam
February 15	The Coast Guard notifies finalists
April 8	Accepted students are notified

Medical Requirements

To be admitted to the Coast Guard Academy you must meet the medical standards for a commissioned officer. The standards shown below are not a complete list, but are intended to give you a general idea of the medical requirements.

1. *Height and Weight*
   Weight must be proportional to height. See the chart in Appendix F.

   Height Range (Men and Women): 5'0" to 6'6"

2. *Eyesight*
   Distant and near vision correctable to 20/20 with uncorrectable vision no worse than 20/200. Refractive error may not exceed +/-5.50 diopters. Normal color vision is required.

3. *Hearing*
   Allowable decibel loss varies from 30 in low frequencies to 55 at high frequencies.

4. *Allergies*
   No severe hay fever. No symptoms of asthma since age 12.

5. *Heart*
   Normal heartbeat. No hypertension or history of cardiovascular problems.

6. *Teeth*
   Numerous unfilled cavities may be a cause for disqualification.

Note: You should take care of any correctable deficiencies before you report for a physical.

Graduation Requirements

You will be expected to:

1. attend the Coast Guard Academy for four years—fall and spring semesters and a training period each summer
2. major in one of these fields of study: Civil Engineering, Electrical Engineering, Marine Engineering, Marine Science, Mathematics, Government, or Management (80% of the cadets must major in a technical area; the remaining 20% can major in either government or management)
3. maintain a 2.0 GPA (C average)
4. successfully pass course requirements and physical and military training; show satisfactory conduct including adherence to an honor code
5. graduate with a Bachelor of Science degree, accept a Regular commission as an ensign in the United States Coast Guard.

Active Duty Requirements

Service Obligation

The minimum service obligation is five years.

Types of Duty

Upon being commissioned as an ensign, graduates proceed to active duty. The majority of the assignments are on board a Coast Guard ship, for example, a cutter conducting search and rescue, an icebreaker in the polar regions, or a buoy tender that maintains navigation aids.

Because Coast Guard ships carry relatively small crews, as an officer you will take on major responsibilities early in your career. Before your first five-year tour of sea duty is completed, it is likely that you will be one of the higher ranking officers on board ship, perhaps even the commanding officer of a small vessel.

The Coast Guard also has an aviation branch you may apply for after one year of sea duty. If selected, you will attend flight training under direction of the Navy. After you receive your wings, you will fly Coast Guard patrol aircraft. Your total service obligation will be extended by the time it takes you to complete flight training.

Although there are no graduate school opportunities directly after you receive your commission, applications are accepted after you serve aboard ship for one year. If you go to graduate school, your active duty time will increase by one year for each year in graduate school.

For more information about the Coast Guard Academy, see your high school guidance counselor or contact:

Director of Admissions
United States Coast Guard Academy
New London, Connecticut 06320

Telephone: 203-444-8500

THE MERCHANT MARINE ACADEMY

Although the Merchant Marine is a civilian service—a privately owned fleet of ships that transport goods all over the world—it is also part of the United States national defense framework. This is because merchant vessels are responsible for importing the strategic materials that are necessary for America's defense as well as for delivering military supplies overseas. The Merchant Marine is known as the "fourth arm of defense" and works closely with the Navy in time of war.

The Merchant Marine is best remembered for its efforts during World War II. At that time the American commercial shipping industry was given the responsibility for transporting thousands of soldiers and millions of pounds of military supplies to U.S. Armed Forces in Europe and throughout the Pacific. It was largely through the work of the Merchant Marine that the United States was able to extend its power across two oceans at the same time.

Beyond the sea-going duties of the Merchant Marine, there is an extensive shore establishment that supports the shipping industry. It includes ports and terminals, shipyards, admiralty lawyers, and engineering and research companies.

Like the Coast Guard, the Merchant Marine does not train officers through an ROTC program. Therefore if you want to graduate from college as a licensed mate or engineer, fully trained and ready to assume duties aboard a commercial ship, the U.S. Merchant Marine Academy at Kings Point, on the North Shore of Long Island in New York, may be the place for you. The primary difference between Kings Point and the service academies is that the other four train officers for the military, while Kings Point graduates officers who will work in a civilian occupation.

In spite of the nonmilitary nature of the Merchant Marine, the Navy maintains close ties with Kings Point. Each student at Kings Point is appointed a midshipman in the Naval Reserve and takes a Naval Science curriculum. Furthermore, graduates of Kings Point are commissioned as officers in the Naval Reserve so they can keep abreast of the current state of affairs in the Navy while they serve in their civilian occupations.

As a midshipman at the Merchant Marine Academy, your college experience will be quite similar to the lifestyle at any of the military academies. You will have a heavy academic load that emphasizes science and engineering, and your nonclassroom activities will be structured along regimental lines. Under the leadership of active-duty Naval officers, this military organization requires that you wear a uniform, adhere to discipline, and follow an honor code.

The Merchant Marine Academy is also like the military service academies in its admission procedures. It too is highly selective, seeking a well-rounded person who combines a strong academic background with characteristics of self-discipline and good citizenship. In a typical year the admissions office at Kings Point receives 2,500 applications. Of the 1,800 who receive nominations, 600 are accepted and about 300 decide to enroll. With a total student body of 1,000 midshipmen, the Merchant Marine Academy is considerably smaller than West Point, Annapolis, or the Air Force Academy, and about the same size as the Coast Guard Academy.

The following are important points about Kings Point.

Costs

The cost of tuition, room and board are paid by the federal government. There is a fee for other expenses of approximately $700. You are not paid while you are at the Merchant Marine Academy but when you take the shipboard part of your academic training you receive an income of approximately $500 per month.

High School Academic Preparation

The Merchant Marine Academy has minimum academic standards for its applicants. You are required to take three years of English, three years of mathematics, and one year of a laboratory science, either physics or chemistry. In addition to these minimum standards, it is desirable if you have a fourth year of math, both physics and chemistry, and courses in mechanical drawing and machine shop.

Eligibility Standards

You need to be a United States citizen, of good moral character, and between 17 and 25 years old. You may be married although midshipmen must reside on campus, apart from their spouses.

Preliminary Screening

You must take the courses mentioned above, rank in the top 40% of your class, and have a combined minimum score of 950 on the SAT or 46 on the math and English sections of the ACT.

Requesting a Nomination

If you meet the minimum qualifications, you can ask for a nomination. Nominations are given by the Congressmen in your home state. During the spring of your junior year in high school, you should write to your Representative and Senators to request a nomination. It is not necessary for you to know your Congressmen nor do you need to have any political connections. Senators and Representatives evaluate the credentials of candidates from their areas and make recommendations to the Kings Point admissions office.

Getting Admitted

When you request a nomination, you should also submit to Kings Point the admission application which includes your high school transcript, a record of your extracurricular activities, results of the SAT or ACT, and letters of recommendation. The Kings Point admissions office will select the best qualified from among those who receive nominations and meet the minimum academic and medical standards. Like the other services, the Merchant Marine Academy looks first at your academic record, but also weighs your leadership potential and strength of character.

Admissions Calendar

Spring of your junior year in high school (preferred) or early senior year	Complete a precandidate questionnaire
Spring of junior year (preferred) or early senior year	Request a nomination
No later than February	Take SAT or ACT
By March 1	Apply
During the Kings Point admissions processing period	Take medical exam
March and April	Kings Point notifies those who receive appointments

Medical Requirements

To be admitted to the Merchant Marine Academy you must meet the medical standards for a commission in the Naval Reserve. The standards shown below are not a complete list, but are intended to give you a general idea of the medical requirements.

1. *Height and Weight*
   Weight must be proportional to height. (See the chart in Appendix F.)

   Height range (men and women): 5'0" to 6'6"

2. *Eyesight*
   Distant and near vision: correctable to 20/20 with uncorrectable vision no worse than 20/100. Refractive error may not exceed +/−5.50 diopters. Normal color vision is required.

3. *Hearing*
   Allowable decibel loss varies from 30 in low frequencies to 60 at high frequencies.

4. *Allergies*
   No severe hay fever. No symptoms of asthma since age 12.

5. *Heart*
   Normal heartbeat. No hypertension or history of cardiovascular problems.

6. *Teeth*
   Numerous unfilled cavities may be a cause for disqualification.

   Note: You should take care of any correctable deficiencies before you report for a physical.

Graduation Requirements

You will be expected to:

1. attend Kings Point for four years—fall and spring semesters and a summer training period each year
2. major in one of four areas: Marine Transportation, Marine Engineering, Dual License (a combination of Marine Transportation and Engineering), or Marine Engineering Systems
3. maintain a 2.0 GPA (C average)
4. participate in two half-year periods at sea on United States merchant vessels
5. successfully pass all required courses (including Naval Science), the U.S. Coast Guard license exam, and physical and military training; show satisfactory conduct including adherence to an honor code
6. graduate with a Bachelor of Science degree and a merchant license, accept a commission in the U.S. Naval Reserve.

After Graduation

As a licensed officer in the Merchant Marine, you are required to serve for at least five years as an employee in the maritime industry of the United States, either on board ship or in another area approved by the Secretary of Transportation. Your first shipboard position will be as a Third Mate or Third Assistant Engineer. Your pay and benefits depend on the contract you sign with your employer. Keep in mind you also will be a member of the Naval Reserve while you go about your civilian occupation. As such, you will be required to attend drills every month and serve two weeks of active duty each year.

Because a Merchant Marine Academy midshipman receives the same kind of military training as a student at Annapolis, a limited number of graduates may choose to become full-time Naval officers and fulfill their five-year service obligation in that manner.

Special Note for Women

The Merchant Marine Academy was the first coeducational academy, accepting women in 1974. Since the Merchant Marine is not a military service, there are no restrictions on the type of duty to which a woman may be assigned. As a Naval Reserve officer, a woman will be subject to the limitations on assignments to combat positions that were already mentioned. However, as a practical matter, Reserve officers are usually far removed from combat and women should encounter very few restrictions in military duty.

For more information, see your high school guidance counselor or contact:

Admissions Office
United States Merchant Marine Academy
Kings Point, New York 11024

Telephone: 516-482-8200

Your high school guidance counselor should be able to tell you who the Kings Point Training Representative is for your area.

THE SERVICE ACADEMIES COMPARED

The following table summarizes important characteristics of the military academies.

	West Point	Annapolis	Air Force	Coast Guard	Merchant Marine
Type of Academy		Military			Civilian, but close connection with the Navy
Eligibility Standards	U.S. citizen, high school graduate, age 17–22, good moral character, no personal convictions against serving in the military, unmarried				The same except age 17–25, may be married
Academic Requirements		None		3 years math, 3 years English	3 years math, 3 years English, 1 year science
Medical Requirements	Same as AROTC scholarship standards	Same as NROTC scholarship standards	Same as AFROTC scholarship except 75% must meet flight training height and vision standards	Similar to NROTC scholarship standards	Same as NROTC scholarship except eyesight standards are more lenient
Scholarship Benefits	Free tuition, room and board. Pay of $500 per month, travel allowance, free flights on military aircraft				Free tuition, room and board. Pay for shipboard training. A $700 charge for other expenses.
Military Requirements	Enlist in the Reserve, pass military training, adhere to discipline standards. May resign prior to end of sophomore year without penalty.				
Graduation Requirements	Attend 4 years, major in approved subject, maintain 2.0 average, pass required courses and physical training. Comply with honor code, graduate with Bachelor of Science degree.				

(continued on next page)

The Service Academies Compared (continued)

	West Point	Annapolis	Air Force	Coast Guard	Merchant Marine
Summer Training	——————————— Attend 4 Summer Sessions ———————————				
Type of Commission	Regular 2nd Lieutenant	Regular Navy Ensign or Marine 2nd Lieutenant	Regular 2nd Lieutenant	Regular Ensign	Licensed as Merchant Marine officer. Commissioned Ensign, Navy Reserve
Length of Active Duty	——————————— Minimum of 5 years ———————————				
Admissions Calendar					
Preliminary Application	—— Spring junior year in high school ——			None	None
Nomination	— Spring junior year or early senior year —			None	Spring junior year or early senior year
Application Deadline	Mar	Feb	Jan	Jan	Mar
Notification	——————————— Fall senior year through the spring senior year ———————————				
Pay and Benefits	——————————— Standard military pay and benefits ———————————				Based on contract with employer

Chapter **4**

Special Programs

In addition to ROTC and the service academies, there are a number of other programs in which the military will pay you money for college in return for a promise by you to become an officer. None of these options requires that you participate in military activities during the academic year. Specific officer training takes place either during the summer or after you graduate from college.

NAVY NUCLEAR PROPULSION OFFICER CANDIDATE PROGRAM

This is a path to a commission for engineering and science majors who want to serve in the nuclear Navy. It is highly selective but those who are chosen receive substantial financial benefits.

You may apply for the Nuclear Propulsion Officer Candidate Program as a sophomore or junior in college. The Navy is looking for math, physics, chemistry or engineering majors with high grade point averages. If accepted, you will be paid a $3,000 bonus and a minimum of $1,000 each month until you graduate.

There are no military requirements while you are in college except to maintain good grades and graduate on time. After receiving your degree, you attend the Navy Officer Candidate School for four months. Upon commissioning, you incur a five-year active duty obligation that begins with six months at nuclear power school, followed by six months at a nuclear "prototype" (a land-based model of a shipboard propulsion system), and attendance at either a submarine school or surface warfare school before reporting to the fleet.

For more information, contact a Navy Recruiting Station.

MARINE CORPS PLATOON LEADERS CLASS

This program is the largest single source of Marine Corps officers and provides a way for you to become a second lieutenant without a time commitment during the academic year. You may apply during any of your first three years in college. As a freshman or sophomore you will attend two six-week training sessions at

Quantico, Virginia. If you are a junior, there is one ten-week session. You are entitled to receive $100 a month for up to three years, a maximum of $2,700 in pay.

A unique aspect of the Platoon Leaders Class is that the time you spend in this program counts towards "longevity" in determining your salary once you become a second lieutenant. For example, if you sign up for the PLC as a college freshman, you will enter the Marine Corps as a second lieutenant with three years of qualifying service. This means you will receive $4,000 more in pay than the officers who come in through other programs.

Upon being commissioned as a second lieutenant, you will first go to Basic School and then either directly to the Fleet Marine Force or to flight training if you have been selected for aviation. There is a special option in the PLC program for students pursuing a law degree. For more information, contact a Marine Corps Officer Selection Office.

ARMED FORCES HEALTH PROFESSIONS SCHOLARSHIP PROGRAM

The Army, Navy, and Air Force offer 5,000 scholarships to students who are attending accredited civilian medical schools in the United States or Puerto Rico. You apply for this program during your senior year in college at the same time you are admitted to medical school. The benefits are tuition and fees, books, and a stipend of approximately $600 per month. Upon matriculation you are commissioned as a second lieutenant or ensign. During your first summer vacation period you receive basic officer training. Each summer thereafter you serve on military active duty for forty-five days. The length of your required service depends on how many years you received the scholarship; the typical obligation is four years.

Note: On page 34 in the Air Force section, there is a description of two- and three-year pre-health profession scholarships for undergraduates enrolled in ROTC. Students who successfully complete this program and are accepted to medical school automatically qualify for the Health Professions Scholarship.

If you would like to know more about this program, contact the Medical Officer Recruiting Office for the service you are interested in. Overall coordination for all three branches takes place in the Office of the Assistant Secretary of Defense (Health Affairs), The Pentagon, Washington, D.C. 20301.

THE UNIFORMED SERVICES UNIVERSITY OF THE HEALTH SCIENCES

This medical education program is similar to the Armed Forces Health Professions Scholarship. The main difference is that, instead of attending a civilian medical school, you enroll at the Uniformed Services University of the Health Sciences in Bethesda, Maryland. You apply as you would to any other medical school. There is no charge for tuition since your education is subsidized by the federal government. All students are paid active duty military officers, normally graduates of ROTC, an academy, or Officer Candidate School. You may also apply as a civilian and be trained as an officer while you are enrolled. Graduates have a seven-year service obligation.

For more information, contact:

Director of Admissions
Uniformed Services University of the Health Sciences
National Naval Medical Center
4301 Jones Bridge Road
Bethesda, Maryland 20014

Telephone: 301-295-3101

AIR FORCE COLLEGE SENIOR ENGINEERING PROGRAM

This is a small program (approximately 75 students are selected each year) for engineering majors who are in their junior or senior year in college.

If you are selected you enlist as an Airman First Class and are paid in that grade (a rate of about $725 per month) until you receive your bachelor's degree. You then go to Officer Training School for about three months. Upon completion you are commissioned as a second lieutenant in the Air Force and begin a four-year service obligation. Your duty assignment will be in the engineering field in which you majored.

5

Weighing the Different Options

Up to this point, *How The Military Will Help You Pay For College* has described the various officer training programs that provide financial aid to help you pay for college. What you have read so far has been a compilation of facts—eligibility standards, scholarship obligations, how to apply, what to expect in college, and the types of jobs available to you after graduation. To complete the picture, what you now need are some "rules of thumb," or general guidelines that will help you figure out which path would be most suitable for you.

CONSIDERING THE ACADEMIES

If you want to be a career military officer, first think about a service academy. Except for relatively minor differences, your undergraduate experience at any of the service academies will be much the same. You will wear a uniform, lead a structured life, go to college virtually all year 'round, receive a very good, technically oriented education, and graduate with a Bachelor of Science degree, all at the government's expense. After graduation you will enter the service well prepared and well motivated to embark on a career. When thinking about which of the academies you want to try for, concentrate mainly on how you see yourself fitting with the type of post-college duty and lifestyle that a particular service offers.

The Merchant Marine Academy is the most distinctive since nearly all graduates become civilian officers either on privately owned ships engaged in commerce or as part of the maritime shore establishment. As an employee of the shipping industry, you are not subject to military regulations and your salary is based on a contract with your employer rather than on the military pay schedule. Even though you are trained to pursue a civilian occupation, there nevertheless is a close connection to the Navy. Upon graduation you will be commissioned as an officer in the Naval Reserve. Although nearly all Merchant Marine Academy ensigns are assigned to the Ready Reserve, and fulfill their service obligation as "Weekend Warriors," you also have the option to join the active duty Navy and become a full-time military officer.

The Coast Guard Academy is the next easiest to separate out. Although the Coast Guard is classified as a military service, it is part of the Department of Transportation, and its primary mission is to save lives and protect property. It does carry out military-like functions, usually during wartime when it comes under the Navy but also in peacetime when it enforces maritime law. As a Coast Guard officer you probably will work from a base in the United States, be assigned to a small ship, and assume considerable responsibility at an early age.

The three large academies, West Point, Annapolis, and Air Force, are quite similar in a number of respects. Their admissions standards are about the same, they are of comparable size, the quality of education is equally strong, graduates are commissioned as Regular officers in a military service that is part of the Department of Defense, and active duty jobs are quite varied with considerable time spent outside the United States. Because of these similarities, you should base your choice among the Army, Navy, Air Force, or Marine Corps on how your abilities and aspirations fit with the type of duty you can expect after graduation rather than on less important differences in location, lifestyle, and academic programs at the academies themselves. To do this most effectively, you should reread the "Types of Duty" section in Chapters 2 and 3, refer to the academies' own publications, and talk with individuals who have served in the military.

CONSIDERING THE ROTC SCHOLARSHIPS

If you are willing to consider a career as a military officer, but aren't quite sure, and you prefer a normal college experience to life at an academy, try for the four-year ROTC scholarship. Choosing the right ROTC program can be even more complicated than deciding among the academies since there are more differences among the ROTC programs than there are among the academies. If you have a strong reason for wanting to be in a particular service, go ahead and try for that ROTC scholarship and plan an academic program that will give you the best chance for selection. If, however, you have no clear preference between the Army, Navy, Air Force, or Marine Corps, you should turn to secondary considerations and ask yourself the following questions.

1. *What is my area of academic interest?*
   If you want to be an engineer you will be attractive to all four services, but the Air Force selects a significantly higher proportion of engineers than the Army or Navy. If you plan to be a liberal arts major, your odds of being selected are better with the Navy and Marine Corps, somewhat less with the Army, and smallest with the Air Force.
2. *How will I do on the medical exam?*
   The main difference among the services is in the vision standards. For non-flying jobs, the Air Force is most lenient. Your correctable eyesight can be worse than 20/20. The Army is next, allowing less than normal vision, provided it is correctable to 20/20. The Navy and Marine Corps, except for a

limited number of waivers, require 20/20 eyesight. You can see what other differences there are in the medical standards by rereading those sections in Chapter 2.

3. *How much time do I want to devote to ROTC during the school year and summer?*

The Army and the Air Force require less of a time commitment than the Navy and Marine Corps. The Army and Air Force Military Science courses total approximately 16 credit hours, and the only other course requirement is one semester of a foreign language. There is one summer training period. Four years of Navy ROTC courses add up to 22–24 credit hours. In addition to a foreign language requirement, Navy midshipmen take math and physics, and Marine Corps option students take Military Affairs and National Security Policy. There are three summer training periods.

4. *How closely do I want my military duty to relate to my academic major?*

The AFROTC scholarship program is designed to attract engineering majors who will have technical jobs after graduation. The Army, Navy and Marine Corps are much more open-minded about what you major in. They are looking for well-rounded well-educated officers who will use their academic background more generally in exercising leadership and management skills.

5. *Do I want to do graduate work before I go on active duty?*

Your chances of going to graduate school prior to entering active duty are higher with the Army and Air Force and less likely with the Navy and Marine Corps.

6. *How important is a Regular commission to me?*

The Air Force ROTC commissions nearly all its second lieutenants as Reserve officers. Therefore, as an Air Force ROTC graduate you will start out on a less advantageous career path than a Regular officer from the Air Force Academy.

The Navy and Marine Corps commission four-year scholarship students as Regular officers, the same designation that Naval Academy graduates receive. This places Naval ROTC graduates on an equal footing with ensigns and second lieutenants from Annapolis.

The Army has three different commissioning alternatives. All West Point graduates and some ROTC graduates go into the Regular Army. Other ROTC graduates are designated Reserve officers and are assigned to four years of active duty, while still others are commissioned as second lieutenants with the National Guard or Army Reserve and go to a six-month Basic Course before becoming "Weekend Warriors." Army ROTC scholarship recipients who fall into this last category have the shortest active duty service requirement of all ROTC scholarship recipients.

There is the possibility that you will decide the four-year ROTC scholarship is the program for you but when you apply you are not accepted. In this case, it would be a good idea to join an ROTC unit when you get to college as a freshman and try for an in-college scholarship as soon as one becomes available. This is a particularly worthwhile strategy if you were classified as an "alternate" when you applied for the four-year ROTC scholarship, because your chance of winning a three-year scholarship is very good.

CONSIDER DEFERRING AN ROTC DECISION

If, as a high school student, you aren't very interested in the military, wait until you get to college to make a decision about joining ROTC. Then you can visit an ROTC unit on campus and decide if you want to join as a nonscholarship student. Should you decide to join, stay with it for at least a semester to see how you get along. If you remain a member of the unit, then think seriously about applying for an in-college scholarship.

OFFICER TRAINING PROGRAMS FOR THOSE ALREADY IN COLLEGE

If you're already in college and the idea of serving as a military officer looks attractive, either visit an ROTC unit on your campus and see what they have to offer or think about joining one of the special officer training programs. As long as you apply by the spring of your sophomore year, you should be eligible for a two-year scholarship program. You make up the first two years of ROTC by attending a summer training camp prior to your junior year. You then join an ROTC unit for your last two years and receive a commission upon graduation. Whether you choose the Army, Navy, Air Force, or Marine Corps depends not only on your personal preference, but also on which service offers a program for you. For example, both Army and Air Force ROTC have two-year scholarships for nursing majors and the Air Force has a program for premedical students.

The Navy Nuclear Propulsion Program, the Marine Corps Platoon Leaders Class, the Armed Forces Health Professions Program, the Uniformed Services University of the Health Sciences, and the Air Force College Senior Engineering Program are all non-ROTC ways a college student can start training to become an officer and receive financial aid at the same time. You can find out more about these programs at a recruiting station.

PART II

Going into the Military First: College Money for Enlisted Servicemembers

The first part of *How The Military Will Help You Pay For College* described officer training opportunities available to college students who enroll in college directly after high school with the intention of becoming an officer, and how the money (either free tuition or direct pay) can be important in helping finance a college education. However, you can also get educational benefits from the military by enlisting in the Army, Navy, Air Force, Marine Corps, or Coast Guard right after high school. When you sign on as a private, seaman or airman, you become eligible for two large sources of aid that will reduce the cost of taking college courses and getting your college degree.

The first category consists of programs you can participate in while you are on active duty, so-called "in-service" education. These range from earning college credit for your military specialty (for example, as a radar technician you can receive credit for completing military electronics school as well as for on-the-job training) or taking courses at a local college with a 75% reduction in tuition.

The second type of college aid available to enlisted servicemembers is "after service" education, part of the New GI Bill which went into effect on July 1, 1985. Under the New GI Bill, the military puts up about $8 for every $1 you contribute toward your college education. This arrangement enables you to build a college savings account that you can draw on after you leave the service.

Besides these two sources of college money that are open to all enlisted servicemembers, there is aid available if you want to move from the enlisted ranks to become an officer. This can be done through ROTC, a service academy, or a special program that leads to a commission.

The five military services are very supportive of continuing education programs as a means to improve your job skills and prepare you for employment in civilian life. In a typical year, military members take approximately 700,000 courses through in-service education programs. It is estimated that the New GI Bill, when fully operational, will provide in excess of $500-million in yearly benefits.

It should be pointed out that Part II focuses on the ways in which the military helps enlisted men and women work towards a college degree. Education programs that are available to officers are mentioned in Part I in a section called "Graduate School Opportunities." The Tuition Assistance program explained in Chapter 7 also is available to officers. Service academy graduates and ROTC scholarship recipients are not eligible for the New GI Bill. Officers who enter the military through other routes, like the special programs and Officer Candidate School, can receive New GI Bill benefits under the same rules that are described in Chapter 8.

If you have further questions about the information presented in this part, you should talk with a military recruiter. Recruiters can describe the options that are available and can look at your credentials and give you advice on which programs fit with your qualifications.

6

Enlisting in the Military—Is It for You?

For many young people in high school, going on to college right away is not a path that appeals to them. Instead, they prefer a break from school by going to work—either by taking a regular civilian job or by enlisting in one of the military services. The Armed Forces know that each year many young men and women weigh this decision and they rely on their recruiting centers to point out the advantages of serving in the military as a "first job" after high school graduation. This is a large undertaking since the military is the largest employer of high school graduates in the United States, "hiring" about 300,000 each year.

There are, of course, many reasons why you might want to join the military, for example, serving your country, learning a job skill, or traveling to different parts of the world. This book tells you about one of them—the opportunity to begin your college education part-time while you are on active duty and then to pay for college when you get out by using the New GI Bill.

As the first step in trying to decide whether the military might be a good first job for you, you should learn more about what it's like to serve as an enlisted man or woman. Although there are some major differences in the missions of the different military services (ranging from the nature of the Marine Corps as a small elite fighting force to the Coast Guard's role of protecting life and property), overall the services have a great deal in common. When it comes to recruiting practices, basic training, types of duty, promotions, and levels of pay, the military branches are quite similar. The rest of this chapter describes what you can expect if you enlist in the Armed Forces.

Joining the Service

The five military services—Army, Navy, Air Force, Marine Corps, and Coast Guard—are looking for the same type of person, a man or woman aged 17 to 35 who is a U.S. citizen or permanent resident, in good physical condition, of good moral character, and motivated to serve his or her country. A high school diploma, although not an absolute requirement, is highly recommended. (Currently about

90% of enlistees have graduated from high school.) All enlistees must also meet minimum standards on a military aptitude test.

After deciding which military service you want to enter, you report to a processing center where you take a medical exam and a series of aptitude tests. These results, combined with your level of education, determine whether you receive a regular assignment or qualify for a special program that includes such features as guaranteed job selection, an enlistment bonus, and accelerated promotion.

When you join the Armed Forces you sign an enlistment contract. The military agrees to provide a job and a salary. In return, you agree to serve for a certain period of time. The contract is for eight years, divided between active duty and Reserve duty. A typical enlistment is for three to six years, although the Army offers a two-year option. After your active duty obligation ends, you spend the rest of the eight years in the Reserves. It is also possible to join the Reserve Forces directly; see page 70.

Training

Whichever service you join, you begin with basic training. Typically this initial exposure to the military consists of 10 weeks of intensive training during which time you engage in physical conditioning, field exercises, and drills and ceremonies. You also learn about military regulations, the use of weapons, and the organization of the military. Beyond general military training, you will be taught specific subjects that are related to the service in which you enlist, such as the practice of seamanship in the Navy and Coast Guard. Basic training consists of a rigorous daily routine that begins at 6:00 a.m. and continues until 10:00 p.m. The schedule is somewhat lighter on weekends but there is little free time available. On occasion you will have the opportunity to receive visitors or leave the training center for a brief period.

After basic training either you go to a technical training school where you are taught a specific skill or you report directly to your duty station for on-the-job training.

Job Assignments

The type of job you have and where you are stationed can range from being a clerk at a base near your home to being a missile technician aboard a ship in the Western Pacific. Not only are there differences among the services themselves, but within any one military branch there is considerable variation depending on the needs of the service, your own qualifications, and your preference for where you would like to be located. On the average, you will spend from 2 to 4 years working in your military job. While you are learning a skill, you will advance in rate and assume more responsibility within the military structure. During this time it is likely that you will be assigned to overseas duty and have the opportunity to visit other parts of the world.

The hundreds of different military occupations have been classified into twelve groups. It is estimated that about 75% of all enlisted jobs have a direct counterpart in the civilian workplace. Here are the twelve areas and examples of jobs within each:

Human Services
    caseworker, counselor, recreation specialist

Media and Public Affairs
    audiovisual specialist, photographer, reporter

Health Care
    dental assistant, nurse, laboratory technician

Engineering, Science, and Technical
    computer programmer, air traffic controller, weather observer

Administration
    recruiter, secretary, payroll specialist

Service
    cook, security policeman, firefighter

Vehicle and Machinery Mechanics
    aircraft mechanic, heating and cooling mechanic, office machine repairer

Electronic and Electrical Equipment Repair
    electronic instrument repairer, power plant electrician, radio equipment repairer

Construction
    carpenter, ironworker, plumber

Machine Operator and Precision Work
    machinist, optician, truckdriver

Transportation and Material Handling
    construction equipment operator, flight engineer, cargo handler

Combat Specialties
    infantryman, combat engineer, artillery crew member

Enlisted Ranks

The following chart shows the rating system (equivalent to pay grades) for enlisted servicemembers and the common titles used by the different branches. Grades E-4 and above are designated NCOs—noncommissioned officers.

Pay Grade and Title

Service	E-1	E-2	E-3	E-4	E-5	E-6	E-7	E-8	E-9
Army	Pvt	Pvt	Pvt 1st Class	Cpl	Sgt	Staff Sgt	Sgt 1st Class	Master Sgt	Sgt Major
Navy	Seaman Recruit	Seaman App	Seaman	PO 3rd Class	PO 2nd Class	PO 1st Class	Chief PO	Senior Chief PO	Master Chief PO
Air Force	Airman Basic	Airman	Airman 1st Class	Sgt	Staff Sgt	Tech Sgt	Master Sgt	Senior Master Sgt	Chief Master Sgt
Marine Corps	Pvt	Pvt 1st Class	Lance Cpl	Cpl	Sgt	Staff Sgt	Gunnery Sgt	Master Sgt	Sgt Major
Coast Guard	Seaman Recruit	Seaman App	Seaman	PO 3rd Class	PO 2nd Class	PO 1st Class	Chief PO	Senior Chief PO.	Master Chief PO

Pvt = Private
Cpl = Corporal
Sgt = Sergeant
App = Apprentice
PO = Petty Officer

Promotions

While there is some variation from service to service, the typical advancement schedule looks like this:

Rate	Total Service Time
From E-1 to E-2	6 months
From E-2 to E-3	1 year
From E-3 to E-4	2 to 2½ years
From E-4 to E-5	3½ to 4 years
E-5 and above	Varies depending on performance and needs of the service.

Promotion to E-2 and E-3 is fairly automatic provided you have a satisfactory training record and receive a recommendation from your commanding officer.

Promotion to E-4 is a competitive process. It depends on your time in grade, and you must pass an advancement test and exhibit skill in your job specialty. Promotion to E-5 usually requires a high school diploma, further demonstration of job proficiency, and approval of a selection board.

Pay and Benefits

They are the same for all five services. See Appendix E.

Special Enlistment Programs

Each service offers a special "track" for highly qualified enlisted men and women. Those who have completed a Junior ROTC program in high school, have experience in critical job areas, or have completed a year or two of college have the greatest chance of being selected. These special programs offer such benefits as:

- assignment to the job specialty you choose
- assignment to a specific geographic location
- delay in reporting to active duty
- an enlistment bonus of up to $8,000
- enlistment at E-2 or E-3 grade rather than as a recruit
- accelerated promotion

Joining the Reserves

While most enlisted servicemembers sign on for a 3- to 6-year term, an alternative is to join the National Guard or Reserve Forces and serve only about six months on active duty for training before joining a Reserve Unit. As a Reservist you are required to drill one weekend a month and go on two weeks of active duty each year until you fulfill your required service obligation, usually 5½ years of drill participation and 2 years in the inactive, or nondrilling, Reserve.

You may hold down a regular civilian job while you participate in the National Guard or Reserves. Your military salary is based on the same schedule as an active duty member but you are only paid for the days you attend drill or go on active duty.

As explained in Chapter 8, as a Reservist you may qualify for education benefits.

Women in the Military

As mentioned previously, the role of women in the military has increased substantially during the past ten years and the services actively encourage women to enlist. The number of women in the military now totals over 200,000, the highest number ever. With the exception of combat positions, nearly all of the jobs mentioned earlier are open to women as well as to men.

7

Earning College Credits on Active Duty

Although you may use the New GI Bill to pay for college courses you take while you are on active duty, it is much more common to save your benefits until you leave the service. Since the military has a number of its own in-service education programs that cost little or nothing, most servicemembers save the money they accumulate under the GI Bill until they complete their tour of duty and enroll in college.

This chapter describes the programs offered by the services that enable you to earn college credit while you are on active duty. These fall into two categories: (1) courses you take on your own during off-duty hours; and (2) credit you receive by demonstrating proficiency in your job specialty.

OFF-DUTY EDUCATION

Opportunities for off-duty education are organized in much the same way by each of the five military services. Each base has an education office that can assist you if you want to enroll in a local college or advance your education without attending class by taking correspondence courses.

For enlisted men and women who want to pursue a degree along traditional lines, the military has made arrangements with a number of colleges to offer flexible academic programs that take into account the unique lifestyle of a servicemember with its time constraints and pattern of frequent reassignments. To accomplish this, the Army, Navy, Marine Corps, and Coast Guard have established an education network called Servicemembers Opportunity Colleges (SOC). The Air Force's program is called the Community College of the Air Force.

Arrangements for servicemembers to receive college credit by correspondence courses and examinations are coordinated by all the services under a program called DANTES (Defense Activity for Non-Traditional Education Support).

In addition to making it easier for you to take courses, either in the classroom or through the mail, the services also provide money for your education in the form of tuition discounts. Under a program called Tuition Assistance, the military pays 75% of the tuition cost. (Depending on rank, time in service and type of course, reimbursement can be as much as 90%.) You may take full advantage of Tuition Assistance while you are in the service and still receive benefits under the New GI Bill after you get out; there is no connection between the two programs.

Each service has a somewhat different way it organizes its off-duty education programs. The variations are described below.

ARMY

Within an overall framework called Army Continuing Education, the Army has divided its off-duty education into two levels called Servicemembers Opportunity Colleges Associate Degree (SOCAD) and Servicemembers Opportunity Colleges (SOC). Both are voluntary, off-duty education programs in which a servicemember takes courses—at a 75% discount—at nearby civilian colleges which have signed up to be part of the SOCAD or SOC network.

You enroll in SOCAD if you want to work toward a two-year (associate) degree. You may take coursework through any one of about 50 accredited colleges offering subjects in 16 academic areas, ranging from accounting to computers to general studies. The colleges that participate in SOCAD have agreed to limit residency requirements, to grant credit for military work experience, to guarantee that course credit can be transferred to another college within the network, and to offer flexible class hours that take into account a servicemember's schedule. These special arrangements are designed to make it possible for you to earn an associate degree while you are in the service. Your degree is granted by the first college in which you enroll. If you are transferred to another base in the middle of your education program, you may enroll at another SOCAD college. The courses you take there will count toward your degree at your "home" institution.

SOC is set up in the same way as SOCAD but it offers courses that can be used to get a bachelor's or graduate degree. So far, the Army has been concentrating its resources on the SOCAD program, but it expects to expand its educational SOC services in the near future.

NAVY

The Navy's commitment to the education of its enlisted men and women is coordinated within a structure called Navy Campus. Navy Campus hires civilian guidance counselors to help you design an education program that meets your goals.

The Navy's Servicemembers Opportunity Colleges is abbreviated SOCNAV. As with the Army, you can earn an associate degree at any one of about 25 SOCNAV colleges. These colleges have agreed to the same kind of flexible academic arrangements that were described under the Army's SOCAD program. SOCNAV participants are eligible for Tuition Assistance so you only have to pay 25% of the tuition cost. SOCNAV may eventually be extended to include bachelor's and graduate degrees.

The Navy also has a Certificate/Degree program (offered primarily through the New York State Regents College) which works in much the same way as SOCNAV except there is no residency requirement at all. Regents College certifies work that you do, primarily by giving credit for your military job skills, thus making it possible for you to get a degree without attending class. This is particularly helpful for Navy personnel who serve on sea duty for extended periods of time.

The Navy Campus guidance counselor also can arrange for you to receive credit for courses taken at a college that doesn't participate in SOCNAV or the Certificate/Degree Program. Such opportunities are worked out individually and depend on your interests.

Finally, the Navy offers an educational opportunity called PACE (Program for Afloat College Education) in which college courses are taught aboard ships assigned to the Navy fleet.

AIR FORCE

The Community College of the Air Force is a program that offers a two-year associate degree in applied science. You can earn this degree, requiring 64 semester hours, by combining on-the-job technical training or attendance at Air Force schools with college courses taken during off-duty hours. There are education centers at Air Force bases where counselors help you enroll at a local college and take placement examinations, and monitor your educational progress. Tuition Assistance covers 75% of the cost of Community College of the Air Force.

Education programs that lead to a bachelor's or graduate degree can also qualify for Tuition Assistance. All Air Force bases offer at least four separate subject areas at the bachelor's level and two graduate disciplines.

MARINE CORPS

The Marine Corps also uses a Servicemembers Opportunity Colleges (SOC) arrangement to help you earn a college degree. SOC in the Marine Corps is structured along the same lines as in the Navy—you can take college-level courses and advance toward a degree under a flexible arrangement that allows for the time constraints of a Marine on active duty.

The Marine Corps also offers a program that lets you attend college full-time—the Degree Completion Program for Staff Non-Commissioned Officers. This arrangement makes it possible for sergeants who had already started their college education to take up to 18 months of leave to finish their degree. Although tuition is not covered, you receive full pay and allowances for your leave period.

COAST GUARD

The Coast Guard also sponsors several off-duty education programs. As with the other branches of the Armed Forces, the Servicemembers Opportunity Colleges (SOC) is the framework under which most of the courses are offered. Depending on funding levels, it is possible to have 100% of your college tuition covered, an even more generous plan than the other services.

In addition, the Coast Guard provides education in certain job specialties. Examples are an Advanced Electronics Technology school that enables senior enlisted servicemembers to pursue a college degree in electronics engineering, and the Physician's Assistant Program, a two-year course of study that leads to a medical certificate and a commission as a Chief Warrant Officer.

DANTES

The education programs described above are designed to make it easy for you to enroll at a local college and take courses at reduced rates. It may be, however, that you can't arrange your work schedule so you can attend class. If this should be the case, you can further your education through correspondence courses and exams. Each of the five services participates in DANTES (Defense Activity for Non-Traditional Education Support). The DANTES program allows you to take tests to advance your level of education, demonstrate job proficiency, or qualify for college admission. The DANTES Independent Study Catalog lists several hundred courses and examinations. Some of the major areas covered are:

- DANTES Subject Standard Tests (DSST). These are academic and vocational exams you take for college credit.

- College-Level Examination Program (CLEP). Through this College Board program you can earn up to 30 semester hours of credit by passing five CLEP general exams.

- Proficiency Examination Program (PEP). This is another credit-by-examination arrangement, similar to CLEP, sponsored by the American College Testing Program.

- Scholastic Aptitude Test (SAT) and American College Testing exam (ACT). These are used primarily to qualify for college admissions but they also are required for entry into officer training programs.

DANTES also includes tests that enable you to earn a high school diploma or have your job skills certified by professional associations.

When there is a fee for taking DANTES courses or examinations, it is usually possible to use the Tuition Assistance program to cover payments.

ON-THE-JOB TRAINING

For all five military branches, the American Council on Education has worked out a system of evaluating how much college credit you can receive for attending a technical training school, performing certain job skills, and passing the Military Occupational Specialty exam. For example, a Navy communications specialist who serves 3 years on active duty can earn 10–15 credit hours through Navy schools, rating examinations, and professional experience.

The American Council on Education publishes the *Guide to the Evaluation of Educational Experiences in the Armed Services,* commonly known as the "Green Book," a listing of more than 400 military specialties for which it recommends that colleges give credit. To find out more about this method of receiving free college credit, talk with the education specialist on your base.

Chapter **8**

Banking College Money While Enlisted: The New GI Bill

It has long been the practice of the U.S. government to reward men and women who serve in the Armed Forces by helping them pay for college after they leave the service. In one form or another this type of educational benefit has existed since World War II. The latest version is called the New GI Bill and is available if you enter one of the five services—Army, Navy, Air Force, Marine Corps, or Coast Guard—after July 1, 1985. It is expected to continue until July 1, 1988, at which time the effectiveness of the program will be reevaluated.

The New GI Bill replaces the Veteran's Educational Assistance Plan (VEAP), the Armed Forces college financial aid program that had existed for the past eight years. From the point of view of the servicemember, the New GI Bill is a better education plan than VEAP because, while the size of the college fund that you can accumulate is about the same, the government contributes a greater share of the total.

You should keep in mind that this latest GI Bill is brand new. Once the military services have a chance to see how well it works, they are likely to ask the Armed Services committees in Congress to make some modifications. When you reach the point where you must decide whether or not to participate, you should check with the education office on your base about the most up-to-date rules.

If you enlisted before July 1, 1985, you may be eligible to receive money for college under either VEAP or the Vietnam era GI Bill. Check with a Veterans Administration office to determine if you have benefits coming to you from one of these two programs.

BENEFITS FOR ACTIVE DUTY SERVICEMEMBERS

The basic principle of the New GI Bill is that you and the government work together to build an education savings account for you to use after you leave the service. To receive these particular benefits you must sign up for a minimum of two years of continuous active duty. Although you are required to make a contribution to your college account, the military's share is far greater. As a result, the payoff to you is quite high and you should think seriously about participating in the New GI Bill when you enlist.

You may use your New GI Bill benefits for many different kinds of educational programs. You may enroll in an accredited college, working toward a two-year associate degree, a four-year bachelor's degree, or a graduate degree. You may also choose vocational or technical courses. Examples of study in the vocational area are welder, tractor/trailer driver, locksmith, and secretary. In the technical category you can study to be a television repairman or a computer programmer. In general there are relatively few restrictions on the types of courses you can take since veterans are encouraged to pursue whatever type of education can help them become productive members of society.

During your first year on active duty, you will automatically have a total of $1,200 ($100 per month for 12 months) deducted from your paycheck to be put into your "education account." If you serve three years or more, the military adds $9,600 for a total of $10,800. If you spend two years on active duty the military contributes $7,800 for a total of $9,000 in your account. At the time you join the service, you may choose not to participate, by "disenrolling." Unless you specify otherwise, the $100 per month payroll deduction will be made automatically.

Later if you attend college full-time, the $10,800 (or the $9,000) is paid to you once the Veterans Administration has approved your program of study at the rate of $300 per month for up to 36 months or $250 per month for up to 36 months, respectively. If you attend college less than full time, your monthly benefits will be reduced proportionately. Although it is most common to use the GI Bill to help pay for college expenses after you leave the military, it is possible to receive the benefits while still serving on active duty, provided you have served at least 2 years.

Your eligibility to receive benefits ends 10 years after you leave the military. You will find a summary of the New GI Bill benefit schedule at the end of this chapter.

The New GI Bill also permits a servicemember to take a leave of absence for up to two years to pursue an educational program. To be eligible you must complete your initial tour of duty and agree to extend your enlistment two years for each year of leave. During your leave period you continue to receive your basic pay while you use your New GI Bill benefits.

THE NEW ARMY COLLEGE FUND

The law that created the New GI Bill permits a service to add money to the basic GI Bill in order to attract servicemembers into areas where there are personnel shortages. While the Navy, Air Force, Marine Corps, and Coast Guard have been able to attract enough volunteers to meet their recruiting quotas, the Army has had some difficulty in filling its critical jobs (about 25% of the total) and therefore has been authorized to establish the New Army College Fund, a program of educational benefits in addition to the New GI Bill.

The New Army College Fund provides a bonus of up to $400 per month over the basic GI Bill benefits. To be eligible you must: (1) begin your military service after July 1, 1985; (2) graduate from high school; (3) score 50 or above on the Armed Forces Qualification Test; (4) enlist in an approved job specialty; (5) enroll in the New GI Bill; and (6) sign on for an active duty tour of at least 2 years (Reservists are not eligible).

The value of the New Army College Fund is $14,400 if you serve 4 years or more, $12,000 if you serve 3 years, and $8,000 if you go on active duty for 2 years.

There are nearly 100 job specialties that can qualify you for the New Army College Fund, mostly in combat assignments such as Infantry, Field Artillery, and Armor, or technical areas such as electronics, air traffic control, and missile systems. Check with an Army recruiter for a current list.

SUPPLEMENTAL BENEFITS

The New GI Bill allows the services to pay supplemental benefits to servicemembers who stay in for more than five years (or two years of active duty and four years of Reserve duty) beyond the length of time needed to qualify for the basic plan. (At the time this book was printed, none of the services had implemented this option.)

BENEFITS FOR MEMBERS OF THE RESERVES

To receive assistance under the New GI Bill it is not necessary for you to join the active duty military for a minimum of two years. There are also payments for members of the Selected Reserve.

You are eligible if you enlist for a 6-year term after July 1, 1985, provided you have completed your active duty training and have a total of 180 days in the Reserves. If you already have a bachelor's degree you do not qualify.

As a full-time student you will receive $140 per month for up to 36 months, a total of $5,040. The payment is reduced proportionately if you attend college less than full time. The Reserve component of the New GI Bill does not require you to make a contribution—100% of the benefits are paid by the government.

Reservists may take the same kinds of courses that were described in the previous section on the New GI Bill for active duty servicemembers.

SUMMARY OF THE NEW GI BILL

	Servicemember Contributes	Government Contributes	Total Benefit	Army Bonus[1]	Total Army Benefit
Active Duty 4 years of service or longer	$1,200	$9,600	$10,800	$14,400	$25,200
3 years of service	$1,200	$9,600	$10,800	$12,000	$22,800
2 years of service	$1,200	$7,800	$ 9,000	$ 8,000	$17,000
Selected Reservists			$ 5,040		

[1] See page 78 for eligibility rules for the Army bonus.

Chapter **9**

Going from Enlisted Servicemember to Officer

The previous chapters in this part of *How The Military Will Help You Pay For College* told you about enlisted education programs that lower the cost of earning college credits, either while you are in the military or after you get out. There are many reasons for wishing to pursue a college degree while you are in the service, an important one being to prepare yourself for a good job in the civilian workforce. It is possible, however, that after a few years as an enlisted servicemember you may decide to stay in the military, but you would like to become an officer. To make such a transition possible, the military has set up a number of programs that will enable you to get your college degree and be commissioned upon graduation. One way to do this is to win an ROTC scholarship or enter a service academy through a special route that is reserved for enlisted servicemembers. The second way is for you to try for one of the special programs that each service offers to highly qualified enlisted men or women who want to become officers.

ROTC SCHOLARSHIPS

Each of the services that offers ROTC—Army, Navy (includes Marine Corps), and Air Force—gives special consideration to enlisted men and women in the selection process.

There are some different eligibility rules for ROTC scholarship candidates who have prior enlisted service. You may request early release (up to thirty days) from active duty in order to enter an ROTC program. The experience that you have already gained in the military will count as credit towards the freshman and sophomore military courses, thus reducing your ROTC workload for the first two years. The age limit, 21 for high school applicants, can be increased by as many as four years depending on the length of your prior service. Perhaps even more important, the financial benefits are significant. In addition to the full tuition and $100 per month you receive from your ROTC scholarship, you also qualify for the New GI Bill benefits. With the ROTC scholarship paying tuition and the GI Bill taking care of room and board costs, it is likely that you will be able to attend college at very little cost.

SERVICE ACADEMIES

As an enlisted man or woman, you may apply to one of the service academies if you meet the basic eligibility standards and are medically qualified. Chapter 3 contains a description of the general admissions process for West Point, Annapolis (includes the Marine Corps), the Air Force Academy, and the Coast Guard Academy.

There is, however, one important difference between the application procedure for an enlisted member of the active duty military or Reserve Forces and that for a high school student.

The three academies that require nominations (West Point, Annapolis, and the Air Force Academy) have each set aside 160 openings for members of the Armed Forces, thus making that process somewhat easier than it is for those who have no military affiliation. Furthermore, if it is determined that you have the potential to become an officer but you need to improve your academic skills, you may be assigned to the academy preparatory school where you will receive an intensive one-year course in English, science, and mathematics. If you do well in preparatory school, you have a good chance of receiving an appointment to an academy.

Since the Coast Guard Academy does not have a nomination procedure nor does it have a preparatory school, an enlisted servicemember interested in attending the Coast Guard Academy follows the same admissions process as any other applicant.

SPECIAL PROGRAMS OF THE SERVICES

NAVY

The Enlisted Commissioning Program is for well-qualified enlisted men and women who already have earned at least 30 college credits. If selected, you will be designated an officer candidate and will attend a six-week Naval Science Institute. You will then affiliate with an NROTC Unit and complete your studies leading to a bachelor's degree. While attending college you receive your enlisted pay and allowances. Although you must pay for tuition, you may use your benefits under the New GI Bill to cover other educational expenses. Upon graduation you will be commissioned as an ensign and report to active duty.

MARINE CORPS

The Marine Corps also offers an opportunity for selected enlisted men and women to become officers. Through the Marine Corps Enlisted Commissioning Program, enlisted servicemembers who qualify may attend a civilian college and work toward a bachelor's degree. After graduation you attend officer candidate school and are commissioned as a second lieutenant upon completion of your program. You receive your regular pay and allowances while you attend college but you must pay for tuition. However, as in the Navy's program, the New GI Bill may be used for tuition and other expenses.

AIR FORCE

Through its Airmen Education and Commissioning Program, the Air Force selects enlisted servicemembers who have already completed at least 45 semester hours of college and provides the means for them to finish their bachelor's degree. In this program, tuition and fees are paid by the Air Force. Upon graduation you will be commissioned as a second lieutenant and assigned to active duty in a job specialty related to your undergraduate studies.

PART III:

Appendixes

These appendixes contain lists of colleges with various ROTC arrangements. Although the information is accurate as of April 1985, the placement of ROTC detachments and the approval of cross-enrollment contracts can vary from year to year. Therefore, as you begin to make specific college plans, you should double check with the service you are interested in to confirm all details.

APPENDIX A: COLLEGES HOSTING ANY ROTC PROGRAM   Page 86

This list, arranged in alphabetical order by state, shows every college that has an ROTC "host unit," which means that the ROTC detachment is located on that campus. This appendix provides a complete overview of ROTC host activity in the United States.

APPENDIX B: ARMY ROTC PROGRAMS   Page 99

This appendix shows the location of each of the three different types of Army ROTC arrangements. Host colleges, the campus where the unit is actually located, are listed in the left column. Cross-enrollments, colleges that allow you to "commute" to a designated host college to participate in Army ROTC, are shown in the right column next to the colleges with which they have an arrangement. Extension centers, branches of a host ROTC unit that has been placed on another campus, are also shown in the right column next to the host college and under the cross-enrollment colleges. Students attending a college with an ROTC extension center thus participate in ROTC on their own campus.

Under current Army ROTC rules, you must be enrolled at a host college to win a four-year scholarship. You may, however, attend any college with any Army ROTC arrangement—host, cross-enrollment, or extension—and compete for a two- or three-year scholarship.

APPENDIX C: NAVY ROTC PROGRAMS   Page 142

This appendix lists colleges that host Navy ROTC programs or have a cross-enrollment arrangement. As with the Army cross-enrollment, this means that students attending cross-enrollment colleges "commute" to the host unit indicated for their ROTC program. You may attend any college on the list and receive a two-, three-, or four-year Navy ROTC scholarship.

APPENDIX D: AIR FORCE ROTC PROGRAMS   Page 149

This appendix lists colleges that host Air Force ROTC programs or have a cross-enrollment arrangement. As with the Army and Navy cross-enrollment, this means that students attending cross-enrollment colleges "commute" to the host college indicated for their ROTC program. You may attend any of the colleges shown and be eligible for a two-, three-, or four-year Air Force ROTC scholarship. (If you attend a two-year college, you must agree to transfer to a four-year institution if your scholarship requires you to do so.)

NOTE: The list of colleges in Appendixes A through D is current as of April 1985. It is naturally subject to change, as new colleges sign ROTC agreements and others terminate their contracts.

APPENDIX E: MILITARY PAY AND BENEFITS   Page 175

By combining base pay and typical supplemental pay, this table shows approximate salary levels for officers and enlisted servicemembers. The base pay rate is the same for each person in a particular category. Supplemental pay and allowances vary among individuals and take into account housing costs, meal expense, assignment to high-cost-of-living areas, and participation in hazardous duty.

APPENDIX F: HEIGHT AND WEIGHT CHART   Page 178
FOR OFFICERS

This appendix is self-explanatory, setting down the relationship between height and weight for officer candidates. As indicated in the notes, the ranges vary somewhat among the different services.

A

Colleges Hosting Any ROTC Program

	Army	Navy	Air Force
Alabama			
Alabama A&M University, Normal	x		
Alabama State University, Montgomery			x
Auburn University, Auburn University	x	x	x
Jacksonville State University, Jacksonville	x		
Marion Military Institute, Marion	x		
Samford University, Birmingham			x
Troy State University, Troy			x
Tuskegee Institute, Tuskegee Institute	x		x
University of Alabama, Birmingham	x		
University of Alabama, University	x		x
University of North Alabama, Florence	x		
University of South Alabama, Mobile	x		
Alaska			
University of Alaska, Fairbanks	x		
Arizona			
Arizona State University, Tempe	x		x
Embry-Riddle Aeronautical University, Prescott			x
Northern Arizona University, Flagstaff	x		x
University of Arizona, Tucson	x	x	x
Arkansas			
Arkansas State University, State University	x		
Arkansas Tech University, Russellville	x		
Henderson State University, Arkadelphia	x		

	Army	Navy	Air Force

Arkansas (continued)

	Army	Navy	Air Force
Ouachita Baptist University, Arkadelphia	x		
Southern Arkansas University, Magnolia	x		
University of Arkansas, Fayetteville	x		x
University of Arkansas, Little Rock	x		
University of Arkansas, Pine Bluff	x		
University of Central Arkansas, Conway	x		

California

	Army	Navy	Air Force
California Polytechnic State University, San Luis Obispo	x		
California State University, Fresno	x		x
California State University, Long Beach			x
California State University, Sacramento			x
Claremont Colleges, Claremont	x		
Loyola Marymount University, Los Angeles			x
San Diego State University, San Diego	x	x	x
San Francisco State University, San Francisco			x
San Jose State University, San Jose	x		x
University of California, Berkeley	x	x	x
University of California, Davis	x		
University of California, Los Angeles	x	x	x
University of California, Santa Barbara	x		
University of San Diego, San Diego		x	
University of San Francisco, San Francisco	x		
University of Santa Clara, Santa Clara	x		
University of Southern California, Los Angeles	x	x	x

Colorado

	Army	Navy	Air Force
Colorado School of Mines, Golden	x		
Colorado State University, Fort Collins	x		x
Metropolitan State College, Denver	x		
University of Colorado, Boulder	x	x	x
University of Colorado, Colorado Springs	x		
University of Northern Colorado, Greeley			x
University of Southern Colorado, Pueblo	x		

Connecticut

	Army	Navy	Air Force
University of Connecticut, Storrs	x		x

Delaware

	Army	Navy	Air Force
University of Delaware, Newark	x		x

	Army	Navy	Air Force
District of Columbia			
Georgetown University, Washington	x		
George Washington University, Washington		x	
Howard University, Washington	x		x
Florida			
Embry-Riddle Aeronautical University, Daytona Beach	x		x
Florida A&M University, Tallahassee	x	x	
Florida Institute of Technology, Melbourne	x		
Florida Southern College, Lakeland	x		
Florida State University, Tallahassee	x		x
Jacksonville University, Jacksonville		x	
Stetson University, DeLand	x		
University of Central Florida, Orlando			x
University of Florida, Gainesville	x	x	x
University of Miami, Coral Gables	x		x
University of South Florida, Tampa	x		x
University of Tampa, Tampa	x		
Georgia			
Augusta College, Augusta	x		
Columbus College, Columbus	x		
Fort Valley State College, Fort Valley	x		
Georgia Institute of Technology, Atlanta	x	x	x
Georgia Military College, Milledgeville	x		
Georgia Southern College, Statesboro	x		
Georgia State University, Atlanta	x		
Mercer University, Macon	x		
North Georgia College, Dahlonega	x		
Savannah State College, Savannah		x	
University of Georgia, Athens	x		x
Valdosta State College, Valdosta			x
Guam			
University of Guam, Mangilao	x		
Hawaii			
University of Hawaii at Manoa, Honolulu	x		x

	Army	Navy	Air Force
Idaho			
Boise State University, Boise	x		
Idaho State University, Pocatello	x		
University of Idaho, Moscow	x	x	
Illinois			
Eastern Illinois University, Charleston	x		
Illinois Institute of Technology, Chicago		x	x
Illinois State University, Normal	x		
Knox College, Galesburg	x		
Loyola University of Chicago, Chicago	x		
Northern Illinois University, DeKalb	x		
Northwestern University, Evanston		x	
Parks College of Saint Louis University, Cahokia			x
Southern Illinois University, Carbondale	x		x
Southern Illinois University, Edwardsville			x
University of Illinois, Chicago	x		
University of Illinois, Urbana	x	x	x
Western Illinois University, Macomb	x		
Wheaton College, Wheaton	x		
Indiana			
Ball State University, Muncie	x		
Indiana University, Bloomington	x		x
Indiana University–Purdue University, Indianapolis	x		
Purdue University, West Lafayette	x	x	x
Rose-Hulman Institute of Technology, Terre Haute	x		
University of Notre Dame, Notre Dame	x	x	x
Iowa			
Iowa State University, Ames	x	x	x
University of Iowa, Iowa City	x		x
Kansas			
Kansas State University, Manhattan	x		x
Pittsburg State University, Pittsburg	x		
University of Kansas, Lawrence	x	x	x
Wichita State University, Wichita	x		
Kentucky			
Eastern Kentucky University, Richmond	x		

	Army	Navy	Air Force
Kentucky (continued)			
Morehead State University, Morehead	x		
Murray State University, Murray	x		
University of Kentucky, Lexington	x		x
University of Louisville, Louisville	x		x
Western Kentucky University, Bowling Green	x		
Louisiana			
Grambling State University, Grambling			x
Louisiana State University and A&M College, Baton Rouge	x		x
Louisiana Tech University, Ruston			x
Loyola University, New Orleans	x		
McNeese State University, Lake Charles	x		
Nicholls State University, Thibodaux	x		
Northeast Louisiana University, Monroe	x		
Northwestern State University of Louisiana, Natchitoches	x		
Southeastern Louisiana University, Hammond	x		
Southern University and A&M College, Baton Rouge	x	x	
Tulane University, New Orleans	x	x	
University of New Orleans, New Orleans	x		x
University of Southwestern Louisiana, Lafayette			x
Maine			
Maine Maritime Academy, Castine		x	
University of Maine, Orono	x		x
University of Southern Maine, Portland	x		
Maryland			
Johns Hopkins University, Baltimore	x		
Loyola College, Baltimore	x		
Morgan State University, Baltimore	x		
University of Maryland, College Park			x
Western Maryland College, Westminster	x		
Massachusetts			
Boston University, Boston	x	x	x
College of the Holy Cross, Worcester		x	x
Massachusetts Institute of Technology, Cambridge	x	x	x

	Army	Navy	Air Force
Massachusetts (continued)			
Northeastern University, Boston	x		
University of Lowell, Lowell			x
University of Massachusetts, Amherst	x		x
Worcester Polytechnic Institute, Worcester	x		
Michigan			
Central Michigan University, Mount Pleasant	x		
Eastern Michigan University, Ypsilanti	x		
Michigan State University, East Lansing	x		x
Michigan Technological University, Houghton	x		x
Northern Michigan University, Marquette	x		
University of Detroit, Detroit	x		
University of Michigan, Ann Arbor	x	x	x
Western Michigan University, Kalamazoo	x		
Minnesota			
Bemidji State University, Bemidji	x		
College of St Thomas, St Paul			x
Mankato State University, Mankato	x		
Saint John's University, Collegeville	x		
University of Minnesota, Duluth			x
University of Minnesota, Minneapolis	x	x	x
Winona State University, Winona	x		
Mississippi			
Alcorn State University, Lorman	x		
Delta State University, Cleveland	x		
Jackson State University, Jackson	x		
Mississippi State University, Mississippi State	x		x
Mississippi Valley State University, Itta Bena			x
University of Mississippi, University	x	x	x
University of Southern Mississippi, Hattiesburg	x		x
Missouri			
Central Missouri State University, Warrensburg	x		
Kemper Military School and College, Boonville	x		
Lincoln University, Jefferson City	x		
Missouri Western State College, St Joseph	x		
Northeast Missouri State University, Kirksville	x		
Northwest Missouri State University, Maryville	x		

	Army	Navy	Air Force
Missouri (continued)			
Southeast Missouri State University, Cape Girardeau			x
Southwest Missouri State University, Springfield	x		
University of Missouri, Columbia	x	x	x
University of Missouri, Rolla	x		x
Washington University, St Louis	x		
Wentworth Military Academy and Junior College, Lexington	x		
Westminster College, Fulton	x		
Montana			
Montana State University, Bozeman	x		x
University of Montana, Missoula	x		
Nebraska			
Creighton University, Omaha	x		
Kearney State College, Kearney	x		
University of Nebraska, Lincoln	x	x	x
University of Nebraska, Omaha			x
Nevada			
University of Nevada, Las Vegas	x		
University of Nevada, Reno	x		
New Hampshire			
University of New Hampshire, Durham	x		x
New Jersey			
New Jersey Institute of Technology, Newark			x
Princeton University, Princeton	x		
Rider College, Lawrenceville	x		
Rutgers University, New Brunswick	x		x
Saint Peter's College, Jersey City	x		
Seton Hall University, South Orange	x		
New Mexico			
Eastern New Mexico University, Portales	x		
New Mexico Military Institute, Roswell	x		
New Mexico State University, Las Cruces	x		x
University of New Mexico, Albuquerque		x	x

	Army	Navy	Air Force
New York			
Canisius College, Buffalo	x		
Clarkson University, Potsdam	x		x
Cornell University, Ithaca	x	x	x
Fordham University, Bronx	x		
Hofstra University, Hempstead	x		
Manhattan College, Riverdale			x
Niagara University, Niagara University	x		
Polytechnic Institute of New York, Brooklyn	x		
Rensselaer Polytechnic Institute, Troy	x	x	x
Rochester Institute of Technology, Rochester	x		
St Bonaventure University, St Bonaventure	x		
St John's University, Jamaica	x		
St Lawrence University, Canton	x		
Siena College, Loudonville	x		
SUNY College, Brockport	x		
SUNY College, Fredonia	x		
SUNY Maritime College, Bronx		x	
Syracuse University, Syracuse	x		x
University of Rochester, Rochester		x	
North Carolina			
Appalachian State University, Boone	x		
Campbell University, Buies Creek	x		
Davidson College, Davidson	x		
Duke University, Durham	x	x	x
East Carolina University, Greenville			x
Fayetteville State University, Fayetteville			x
North Carolina A&T State University, Greensboro	x		x
North Carolina State University, Raleigh	x		x
Saint Augustine's College, Raleigh	x		
University of North Carolina, Chapel Hill		x	x
University of North Carolina, Charlotte			x
Wake Forest University, Winston-Salem	x		
Western Carolina University, Cullowhee	x		
North Dakota			
North Dakota State University, Fargo	x		x
University of North Dakota, Grand Forks	x		
Ohio			
Bowling Green State University, Bowling Green	x		x

	Army	Navy	Air Force
Ohio (continued)			
Central State University, Wilberforce	x		
John Carroll University, University Heights	x		
Kent State University, Kent	x		x
Miami University, Oxford		x	x
Ohio State University, Columbus	x	x	x
Ohio University, Athens	x		x
University of Akron, Akron	x		x
University of Cincinnati, Cincinnati	x		x
University of Dayton, Dayton	x		
University of Toledo, Toledo	x		
Wright State University, Dayton			x
Xavier University, Cincinnati	x		
Youngstown State University, Youngstown	x		
Oklahoma			
Cameron University, Lawton	x		
Central State University, Edmond	x		
East Central Oklahoma State University, Ada	x		
Northwestern Oklahoma State University, Alva	x		
Oklahoma State University, Stillwater	x		x
Southwestern Oklahoma State University, Weatherford	x		
University of Oklahoma, Norman	x	x	x
Oregon			
Oregon State University, Corvallis	x	x	x
University of Oregon, Eugene	x		
University of Portland, Portland			x
Pennsylvania			
Bucknell University, Lewisburg	x		
Carnegie-Mellon University, Pittsburgh	x		x
Clarion University of Pennsylvania, Clarion	x		
Dickinson College, Carlisle	x		
Drexel University, Philadelphia	x		
Duquesne University, Pittsburgh	x		
Gannon University, Erie	x		
Gettysburg College, Gettysburg	x		
Grove City College, Grove City			x
Indiana University of Pennsylvania, Indiana	x		
Lafayette College, Easton	x		

	Army	Navy	Air Force
Pennsylvania (continued)			
La Salle University, Philadelphia	x		
Lehigh University, Bethlehem	x		x
Pennsylvania State University, University Park	x	x	x
Saint Joseph's University, Philadelphia			x
Shippensburg University of Pennsylvania, Shippensburg	x		
Temple University, Philadelphia	x		
University of Pennsylvania, Philadelphia	x	x	
University of Pittsburgh, Pittsburgh	x		x
University of Scranton, Scranton	x		
Valley Forge Military Junior College, Wayne	x		
Villanova University, Villanova		x	
Washington and Jefferson College, Washington	x		
Widener University, Chester	x		
Wilkes College, Wilkes-Barre			x
Puerto Rico			
University of Puerto Rico, Mayagüez	x		x
University of Puerto Rico, Río Piedras	x		x
Rhode Island			
Providence College, Providence	x		
University of Rhode Island, Kingston	x		
South Carolina			
Baptist College, Charleston			x
The Citadel, Charleston (men only)	x	x	x
Clemson University, Clemson	x		x
Furman University, Greenville	x		
Presbyterian College, Clinton	x		
South Carolina State College, Orangeburg	x		
University of South Carolina, Columbia	x	x	x
Wofford College, Spartanburg	x		
South Dakota			
South Dakota School of Mines and Technology, Rapid City	x		
South Dakota State University, Brookings	x		x
University of South Dakota, Vermillion	x		

	Army	Navy	Air Force
Tennessee			
Austin Peay State University, Clarksville	x		
Carson-Newman College, Jefferson City	x		
East Tennessee State University, Johnson City	x		
Memphis State University, Memphis	x	x	x
Middle Tennessee State University, Murfreesboro	x		
Tennessee State University, Nashville			x
Tennessee Technological University, Cookeville	x		
University of Tennessee, Chattanooga	x		
University of Tennessee, Knoxville	x		x
University of Tennessee, Martin	x		
Vanderbilt University, Nashville	x	x	
Texas			
Angelo State University, San Angelo			x
Baylor University, Waco			x
Bishop College, Dallas	x		
East Texas State University, Commerce			x
Hardin-Simmons University, Abilene	x		
Midwestern State University, Wichita Falls	x		
North Texas State University, Denton			x
Pan American University, Edinburg	x		
Prairie View A&M University, Prairie View	x	x	
Rice University, Houston	x	x	
St Mary's University, San Antonio	x		
Sam Houston State University, Huntsville	x		
Southwest Texas State University, San Marcos			x
Stephen F Austin State University, Nacogdoches	x		
Texas A&I University, Kingsville	x		
Texas A&M University, College Station	x	x	x
Texas Christian University, Fort Worth	x		x
Texas Tech University, Lubbock	x	x	x
Trinity University, San Antonio	x		
University of Houston, Houston	x		
University of Texas, Arlington	x		
University of Texas, Austin	x	x	x
University of Texas, El Paso	x		
University of Texas, San Antonio	x		
West Texas State University, Canyon	x		
Utah			
Brigham Young University, Provo	x		x
University of Utah, Salt Lake City	x	x	x

	Army	Navy	Air Force
Utah (continued)			
Utah State University, Logan	x		x
Weber State College, Ogden	x		
Vermont			
Norwich University, Northfield	x	x	x
Saint Michael's College, Winooski			x
University of Vermont, Burlington	x		
Virginia			
College of William and Mary, Williamsburg	x		
Hampton University, Hampton	x	x	
James Madison University, Harrisonburg	x		
Norfolk State University, Norfolk	x	x	
Old Dominion University, Norfolk	x	x	
University of Richmond, Richmond	x		
University of Virginia, Charlottesville	x	x	x
Virginia Military Institute, Lexington (men only)	x	x	x
Virginia Polytechnic Institute and State University, Blacksburg	x	x	x
Virginia State University, Petersburg	x		
Washington and Lee University, Lexington	x		
Washington			
Central Washington University, Ellensburg			x
Eastern Washington University, Cheney	x		
Gonzaga University, Spokane	x		
Seattle University, Seattle	x		
University of Puget Sound, Tacoma			x
University of Washington, Seattle	x	x	x
Washington State University, Pullman	x		x
West Virginia			
Marshall University, Huntington	x		
West Virginia State College, Institute	x		
West Virginia University, Morgantown	x		x
Wisconsin			
Marquette University, Milwaukee	x	x	
Ripon College, Ripon	x		
St Norbert College, De Pere	x		

	Army	Navy	Air Force

Wisconsin (continued)

	Army	Navy	Air Force
University of Wisconsin, La Crosse	x		
University of Wisconsin, Madison	x	x	x
University of Wisconsin, Milwaukee	x		
University of Wisconsin, Oshkosh	x		
University of Wisconsin, Platteville	x		
University of Wisconsin, Stevens Point	x		
University of Wisconsin, Superior			x
University of Wisconsin, Whitewater	x		

Wyoming

	Army	Navy	Air Force
University of Wyoming, Laramie	x		x

Army ROTC Programs

HOST COLLEGES	CROSS-ENROLLMENTS AND EXTENSIONS
Alabama	
Alabama A&M University, Normal	Cross-Enrollments John C. Calhoun State Community College, Decatur University of Alabama, Huntsville
Auburn University, Auburn University	Cross-Enrollments Alabama State University, Montgomery Troy State University, Montgomery Extension Auburn University, Montgomery
Jacksonville State University, Jacksonville	Cross-Enrollment Gadsden State Junior College, Gadsden
Marion Military Institute, Marion	
Tuskegee Institute, Tuskegee Institute	
University of Alabama, Birmingham	Cross-Enrollments Birmingham-Southern College, Birmingham Jefferson Davis State Junior College, Brewton Miles College, Birmingham Samford University, Birmingham University of Montevallo, Montevallo
University of Alabama, University	Cross-Enrollment Stillman College, Tuscaloosa
University of North Alabama, Florence	

HOST COLLEGES	CROSS-ENROLLMENTS AND EXTENSIONS

Alabama (continued)

University of South Alabama, Mobile	**Cross-Enrollments** James H. Faulkner State Junior College, Bay Minette Mobile College, Mobile S D Bishop State Junior College, Mobile Spring Hill College, Mobile

Alaska

University of Alaska, Fairbanks	

Arizona

Arizona State University, Tempe	**Cross-Enrollments** Glendale Community College, Glendale Mesa Community College, Mesa Phoenix College, Phoenix Scottsdale Community College, Scottsdale
Northern Arizona University, Flagstaff	
University of Arizona, Tucson	**Cross-Enrollment** Pima Community College, Tucson

Arkansas

Arkansas State University, State University	
Arkansas Tech University, Russellville	**Cross-Enrollment** College of the Ozarks, Clarksville
Henderson State University, Arkadelphia	
Ouachita Baptist University, Arkadelphia	
Southern Arkansas University, Magnolia	
University of Arkansas, Fayetteville	**Extension** Northeastern Oklahoma State University, Tahlequah (OK)
University of Arkansas, Little Rock	**Cross-Enrollment** Philander Smith College, Little Rock

HOST COLLEGES	CROSS-ENROLLMENTS AND EXTENSIONS

Arkansas (continued)

	Extension
University of Arkansas, Pine Bluff	University of Arkansas, Monticello

	Cross-Enrollments
University of Central Arkansas, Conway	Central Baptist College, Conway
	Hendrix College, Conway

California

	Cross-Enrollments
California Polytechnic State University, San Luis Obispo	Allan Hancock College, Santa Maria
	Cuesta College, San Luis Obispo

California State University, Fresno	

	Cross-Enrollments
Claremont Colleges, Claremont	California State University, Los Angeles
	Chaffey College, Alta Loma
	College of the Desert, Palm Desert
	Crafton Hills College, Yucaipa
	Mt San Antonio College, Walnut
	Riverside City College, Riverside
	San Bernardino Valley College, San Bernardino
	University of California, Riverside
	University of La Verne, La Verne
	University of Redlands, Redlands
	Victor Valley College, Victorville
	Extensions
	California State College, San Bernardino
	California State Polytechnic University, Pomona
	California State University, Fullerton

	Cross-Enrollments
San Diego State University, San Diego	Coleman College, La Mesa
	Grossmont College, El Cajon
	National University, San Diego
	Palomar College, San Marcos
	Point Loma Nazarene College, San Diego
	San Diego City College, San Diego
	San Diego Mesa College, San Diego
	Southwestern College, Chula Vista

HOST COLLEGES	CROSS-ENROLLMENTS AND EXTENSIONS

California (continued)

	Cross-Enrollments University of California, San Diego University of San Diego, San Diego
San Jose State University, San Jose	Cross-Enrollments De Anza College, Cupertino Evergreen Valley College, San Jose Foothill College, Los Altos Hills Mission College, Santa Clara Monterey Peninsula College, Monterey Ohlone College, Fremont West Valley College, Saratoga

University of California, Berkeley	Cross-Enrollments
	California State University, Hayward
	Chabot College, Hayward
	College of Alameda, Alameda
	Contra Costa College, San Pablo
	Diablo Valley College, Pleasant Hill
	Merritt College, Oakland
	Saint Mary's College of California,
	    Moraga
	Solano Community College,
	    Suisun City

University of California, Davis	Cross-Enrollments California State University, Chico California State University, Sacramento

University of California, Los Angeles	Cross-Enrollments
	California State University,
	    Dominguez Hills, Carson
	California State University, Los Angeles
	California State University, Northridge
	College of the Canyons, Valencia
	Glendale Community College, Glendale
	Los Angeles City College, Los Angeles
	Los Angeles Pierce College,
	    Woodland Hills
	Los Angeles Trade-Technical College,
	    Los Angeles
	Los Angeles Valley College, Van Nuys
	Pepperdine University, Malibu
	Santa Monica College, Santa Monica

HOST COLLEGES	CROSS-ENROLLMENTS AND EXTENSIONS

California (continued)

	Cross-Enrollments University of California, Irvine **Extension** California State University, Long Beach
University of California, Santa Barbara	**Cross-Enrollments** California Lutheran College, Thousand Oaks California State University, Northridge

University of San Francisco,
    San Francisco
	Cross-Enrollments
	City College of San Francisco,
	    San Francisco
	College of San Mateo, San Mateo
	Marin Community College, Kentfield
	Saint Mary's College of California,
	    Moraga
	San Francisco State University,
	    San Francisco
	Skyline College, San Bruno

University of Santa Clara, Santa Clara	**Cross-Enrollment** Stanford University, Stanford
University of Southern California, Los Angeles	**Cross-Enrollment** Mount St Mary's College, Los Angeles

Colorado

Colorado School of Mines, Golden	**Extension** Mesa College, Grand Junction
Colorado State University, Fort Collins	**Cross-Enrollment** University of Northern Colorado, Greeley
Metropolitan State College, Denver	**Cross-Enrollments** Loretto Heights College, Denver Rockmont College, Denver University of Colorado, Denver University of Colorado Health Sciences Center, Denver University of Denver, Denver
University of Colorado, Boulder	

HOST COLLEGES	CROSS-ENROLLMENTS AND EXTENSIONS

Colorado (continued)

University of Colorado, Colorado Springs	**Cross-Enrollments** Colorado College, Colorado Springs Colorado Technical College, Colorado Springs Pikes Peak Community College, Colorado Springs
University of Southern Colorado, Pueblo	**Cross-Enrollment** Adams State College, Alamosa

Connecticut

University of Connecticut, Storrs	**Cross-Enrollments** Central Connecticut State University, New Britain Eastern Connecticut State University, Willimantic Fairfield University, Fairfield Northwestern Connecticut Community College, Winsted Sacred Heart University, Bridgeport South Central Community College, New Haven Southern Connecticut State University, New Haven Trinity College, Hartford University of Hartford, West Hartford University of New Haven, West Haven Western Connecticut State University, Danbury Yale University, New Haven **Extensions** University of Bridgeport, Bridgeport University of Connecticut, West Hartford

Delaware

University of Delaware, Newark	**Cross-Enrollments** Delaware State College, Dover Lincoln University, Lincoln University (PA)

HOST COLLEGES	CROSS-ENROLLMENTS AND EXTENSIONS

Delaware (continued)

	Extension Salisbury State College, Salisbury (MD)

District of Columbia

Georgetown University, Washington	Cross-Enrollments American University, Washington Catholic University of America, Washington George Washington University, Washington Marymount College of Virginia, Arlington (VA) Extension George Mason University, Fairfax (VA)
Howard University, Washington	Cross-Enrollments Capitol Institute of Technology, Laurel (MD) Catholic University of America, Washington George Washington University, Washington Prince George's Community College, Largo (MD) Salisbury State College, Salisbury (MD) University of Maryland, College Park (MD) University of the District of Columbia, Washington Extension Bowie State College, Bowie (MD)

Florida

Embry-Riddle Aeronautical University, Daytona Beach	Cross-Enrollments Bethune-Cookman College, Daytona Beach Daytona Beach Community College, Daytona Beach
Florida A&M University, Tallahassee	

HOST COLLEGES	CROSS-ENROLLMENTS AND EXTENSIONS

Florida (continued)

Florida Institute of Technology, Melbourne	**Cross-Enrollments** Brevard Community College, Cocoa Rollins College, Winter Park University of Central Florida, Orlando
Florida Southern College, Lakeland	**Cross-Enrollments** Hillsborough Community College, Tampa Polk Community College, Winter Haven Southeastern College of the Assemblies of God, Lakeland Webber College, Babson Park
Florida State University, Tallahassee	**Cross-Enrollments** Gulf Coast Community College, Panama City Pensacola Junior College, Pensacola Tallahassee Community College, Tallahassee **Extension** University of West Florida, Pensacola
Stetson University, DeLand	**Extension** University of Central Florida, Orlando
University of Florida, Gainesville	**Cross-Enrollments** Florida Junior College, Jacksonville Jacksonville University, Jacksonville Sante Fe Community College, Gainesville **Extension** University of North Florida, Jacksonville
University of Miami, Coral Gables	**Cross-Enrollments** Broward Community College, Fort Lauderdale Florida Atlantic University, Boca Raton Florida International University, Miami Florida Memorial College, Miami Miami-Dade Community College, Miami

HOST COLLEGES	CROSS-ENROLLMENTS AND EXTENSIONS
Florida (continued)	
	Cross-Enrollments St Thomas of Villanova University, Miami
University of South Florida, Tampa	**Cross-Enrollments** Eckerd College, St Petersburg St Petersburg Junior College, St Petersburg **Extensions** Saint Leo College, Saint Leo University of South Florida, Tampa
University of Tampa, Tampa	**Cross-Enrollment** Hillsborough Community College, Tampa
Georgia	
Augusta College, Augusta	**Cross-Enrollments** Paine College, Augusta University of South Carolina, Aiken (SC)
Columbus College, Columbus	**Cross-Enrollment** Chattahoochee Valley State Community College, Phenix City (AL)
Fort Valley State College, Fort Valley	**Extension** Albany State College, Albany
Georgia Institute of Technology, Atlanta	**Cross-Enrollments** Clark College, Atlanta Emory University, Atlanta Floyd Junior College, Rome Kennesaw College, Marietta Morehouse College, Atlanta Morris Brown College, Atlanta Shorter College, Rome Spelman College, Atlanta **Extension** Berry College, Mount Berry
Georgia Military College, Milledgeville	**Cross-Enrollment** Georgia College, Milledgeville

HOST COLLEGES	CROSS-ENROLLMENTS AND EXTENSIONS

Georgia (continued)

Georgia Southern College, Statesboro	**Cross-Enrollments** Emanuel County Junior College, Swainsboro Savannah State College, Savannah **Extension** Armstrong State College, Savannah
Georgia State University, Atlanta	**Cross-Enrollments** Clayton Junior College, Morrow DeKalb Community College, Clarkston West Georgia College, Carrollton
Mercer University, Macon	**Cross-Enrollment** Middle Georgia College, Cochran **Extension** Georgia Southwestern College, Americus
North Georgia College, Dahlonega	
University of Georgia, Athens	**Cross-Enrollments** Gainesville Junior College, Gainesville Truett-McConnell College, Cleveland

Guam

University of Guam, Mangilao	

Hawaii

University of Hawaii at Manoa, Honolulu	**Cross-Enrollments** Brigham Young University, Laie, Oahu Chaminade University, Honolulu Hawaii Pacific College, Honolulu University of Hawaii at Manoa, Honolulu University of Hawaii–Kapiolani Community College, Honolulu University of Hawaii–Leeward Community College, Pearl City University of Hawaii–West Oahu College, Pearl City

Idaho

Boise State University, Boise	**Cross-Enrollments** Northwest Nazarene College, Nampa

HOST COLLEGES	CROSS-ENROLLMENTS AND EXTENSIONS

Idaho (continued)

	Cross-Enrollments Treasure Valley Community College, Ontario (OR)
Idaho State University, Pocatello	**Cross-Enrollments** College of Southern Idaho, Twin Falls Ricks College, Rexburg
University of Idaho, Moscow	**Cross-Enrollment** Lewis-Clark State College, Lewiston

Illinois

Eastern Illinois University, Charleston	
Illinois State University, Normal	
Knox College, Galesburg	**Cross-Enrollment** Monmouth College, Monmouth **Extension** Bradley University, Peoria
Loyola University of Chicago, Chicago	**Cross-Enrollments** DePaul University, Chicago DeVry Institute of Technology, Chicago Illinois Institute of Technology, Chicago Northeastern Illinois University, Chicago Northwestern University, Evanston University of Chicago, Chicago
Northern Illinois University, De Kalb	
Southern Illinois University, Carbondale	**Cross-Enrollment** Southeast Missouri State University, Cape Girardeau (MO)
University of Illinois, Chicago	**Cross-Enrollments** City Colleges of Chicago, Loop College, Chicago City Colleges of Chicago, Malcolm X College, Chicago Rush University, Chicago University of Illinois, Health Sciences Center, Chicago **Extension** Chicago State University, Chicago

HOST COLLEGES	CROSS-ENROLLMENTS AND EXTENSIONS

Illinois (continued)

University of Illinois, Urbana	**Cross-Enrollment** Parkland College, Urbana
Western Illinois University, Macomb	**Cross-Enrollment** Black Hawk College, Moline

Wheaton College, Wheaton	**Cross-Enrollments**
	 College of DuPage, Glen Ellyn
	 DeVry Institute of Technology, Chicago
	 Governors State University,
	     University Park
	 Illinois Benedictine College, Lisle
	 Moraine Valley Community College,
	     Palos Hills
	 Olivet Nazarene College, Kankakee

Indiana

Ball State University, Muncie	**Cross-Enrollment** Indiana University–Purdue University, Fort Wayne
Indiana University, Bloomington	**Extension** Indiana University Southeast, New Albany

Indiana University–Purdue University,
     Indianapolis
	Cross-Enrollments
	 Franklin College of Indiana, Franklin
	 Indiana Central University,
	     Indianapolis

Purdue University, West Lafayette	
Rose-Hulman Institute of Technology, Terre Haute	**Cross-Enrollments** DePauw University, Greencastle Indiana State University, Terre Haute Vincennes University, Vincennes
University of Notre Dame, Notre Dame	**Cross-Enrollments** Holy Cross Junior College, Notre Dame Indiana University, South Bend Saint Mary's College, Notre Dame

Iowa

Iowa State University, Ames	**Cross-Enrollments** Des Moines Area Community College, Ankeny

HOST COLLEGES	CROSS-ENROLLMENTS AND EXTENSIONS

Iowa (continued)

	Cross-Enrollments Grand View College, Des Moines **Extension** Drake University, Des Moines

University of Iowa, Iowa City	**Cross-Enrollments**
	Coe College, Cedar Rapids
	Kirkwood Community College,
	    Cedar Rapids
	Extension
	University of Northern Iowa,
	    Cedar Falls

Kansas

Kansas State University, Manhattan	**Cross-Enrollment** Washburn University, Topeka
Pittsburg State University, Pittsburg	**Cross-Enrollments** Fort Scott Community College, Fort Scott Labette Community College, Parsons
University of Kansas, Lawrence	**Cross-Enrollments** Baker University, Baldwin City Washburn University, Topeka **Extension** Emporia State University, Emporia

Wichita State University, Wichita	**Cross-Enrollment**
	Dodge City Community College,
	    Dodge City
	Extensions
	Fort Hays State University, Hays
	Garden City Community College,
	    Garden City

Kentucky

Eastern Kentucky University, Richmond	**Extension** Cumberland College, Williamsburg
Morehead State University, Morehead	
Murray State University, Murray	

HOST COLLEGES	CROSS-ENROLLMENTS AND EXTENSIONS

Kentucky (continued)

University of Kentucky, Lexington	**Cross-Enrollments** Centre College, Danville Georgetown College, Georgetown Transylvania University, Lexington **Extension** Kentucky State University, Frankfort
University of Louisville, Louisville	
Western Kentucky University, Bowling Green	

Louisiana

Louisiana State University and A&M College, Baton Rouge	**Extension** Louisiana State University, Alexandria
Loyola University, New Orleans	

McNeese State University,
    Lake Charles
	Cross-Enrollment
	University of Southwestern Louisiana,
	    Lafayette
	Extension
	Lamar University, Beaumont (TX)

Nicholls State University, Thibodaux	
Northeast Louisiana University, Monroe	**Extension** Grambling State University, Grambling

Northwestern State University of
    Louisiana, Natchitoches
	Extensions
	Centenary College of Louisiana,
	    Shreveport
	Louisiana College, Pineville
	Louisiana State University,
	    Shreveport

Southeastern Louisiana University, Hammond	
Southern University and A&M College, Baton Rouge	
Tulane University, New Orleans	**Cross-Enrollments** Louisiana State University Medical Center, New Orleans Southern University, New Orleans

HOST COLLEGES	CROSS-ENROLLMENTS AND EXTENSIONS
Louisiana (continued)	
	Extensions Dillard University, New Orleans Xavier University of Louisiana, New Orleans
University of New Orleans, New Orleans	
Maine	
University of Maine, Orono	
University of Southern Maine, Portland	**Cross-Enrollment** Saint Joseph's College, North Windham
Maryland	
Johns Hopkins University, Baltimore	**Cross-Enrollments** Anne Arundel Community College, Arnold Community College of Baltimore, Baltimore Coppin State College, Baltimore Goucher College, Towson Maryland Institute, College of Art, Baltimore Towson State University, Towson University of Baltimore, Baltimore University of Maryland Baltimore County, Baltimore University of Maryland, College Park
Loyola College, Baltimore	**Cross-Enrollments** Catonsville Community College, Catonsville College of Notre Dame of Maryland, Baltimore Community College of Baltimore, Baltimore Essex Community College, Baltimore Harford Community College, Bel Air Towson State University, Towson
Morgan State University, Baltimore	**Cross-Enrollment** Catonsville Community College, Catonsville

HOST COLLEGES	CROSS-ENROLLMENTS AND EXTENSIONS

Maryland (continued)

	Cross-Enrollments
Western Maryland College, Westminster	Catonsville Community College, Catonsville
	Frederick Community College, Frederick
	Hood College, Frederick
	Shepherd College, Shepherdstown (WV)
	Towson State University, Towson
	University of Maryland Baltimore County, Baltimore
	University of Maryland, College Park
	Extensions
	Bowie State College, Bowie
	Frostburg State College, Frostburg
	Mount Saint Mary's College, Emmitsburg
	Salisbury State College, Salisbury

Massachusetts

	Cross-Enrollments
Boston University, Boston	Babson College, Babson Park
	Bentley College, Waltham
	Bridgewater State College, Bridgewater
	Framingham State College, Framingham
	Massasoit Community College, Brockton
	Southeastern Massachusetts University, North Dartmouth
	Extension
	Stonehill College, North Easton
	Cross-Enrollments
Massachusetts Institute of Technology, Cambridge	Harvard University, Cambridge
	Tufts University, Medford
	Wellesley College, Wellesley
	Cross-Enrollments
Northeastern University, Boston	Boston College, Chestnut Hill
	Massachusetts College of Art, Boston

HOST COLLEGES

**CROSS-ENROLLMENTS
AND EXTENSIONS**

Massachusetts (continued)

	Cross-Enrollments
	Massachusetts College of Pharmacy and
	    Allied Health Sciences, Boston
	Merrimack College, North Andover
	Middlesex Community College,
	    Bedford
	North Shore Community College,
	    Beverly
	Simmons College, Boston
	University of Lowell, Lowell
	University of Massachusetts, Boston
	Wentworth Institute of Technology,
	    Boston
	Extensions
	Salem State College, Salem
	Suffolk University, Boston

University of Massachusetts, Amherst	**Cross-Enrollments**
	American International College,
	    Springfield
	Holyoke Community College, Holyoke
	Westfield State College, Westfield
	Extension
	Western New England College,
	    Springfield

Worcester Polytechnic Institute,
    Worcester
	Cross-Enrollments
	Anna Maria College, Paxton
	Assumption College, Worcester
	Central New England College,
	    Worcester
	Clark University, Worcester
	College of the Holy Cross, Worcester
	Framingham State College,
	    Framingham
	Hellenic College, Brookline
	Mount Wachusett Community College,
	    Gardner
	Nichols College, Dudley
	University of Lowell, Lowell
	Worcester State College, Worcester
	Extension
	Fitchburg State College, Fitchburg

HOST COLLEGES	CROSS-ENROLLMENTS AND EXTENSIONS

Michigan

Central Michigan University, Mount Pleasant	Cross-Enrollments Alma College, Alma Kirtland Community College, Roscommon Northwood Institute, Midland Saginaw Valley State College, University Center
Eastern Michigan University, Ypsilanti	
Michigan State University, East Lansing	Cross-Enrollment Lansing Community College, Lansing
Michigan Technological University, Houghton	
Northern Michigan University, Marquette	
University of Detroit, Detroit	Cross-Enrollments Henry Ford Community College, Dearborn Macomb Community College, Warren Madonna College, Livonia Mercy College of Detroit, Detroit Oakland Community College, Bloomfield Hills Oakland University, Rochester Schoolcraft College, Livonia Walsh College of Accountancy and Business Administration, Troy Wayne County Community College, Detroit Wayne State University, Detroit Extension Lawrence Institute of Technology, Southfield
University of Michigan, Ann Arbor	Cross-Enrollments Adrian College, Adrian University of Michigan, Dearborn
Western Michigan University, Kalamazoo	Cross-Enrollments Grand Rapids Baptist College and Seminary, Grand Rapids Grand Valley State College, Allendale

HOST COLLEGES

CROSS-ENROLLMENTS
AND EXTENSIONS

Minnesota

Bemidji State University, Bemidji

Mankato State University, Mankato

Cross-Enrollments
Bethany Lutheran College, Mankato
Gustavus Adolphus College, St Peter

Saint John's University, Collegeville

Cross-Enrollments
College of Saint Benedict,
Saint Joseph
Moorhead State University, Moorhead
St Cloud State University, St Cloud

University of Minnesota, Minneapolis

Cross-Enrollments
Anoka-Ramsey Community College,
Coon Rapids
College of St Thomas, St Paul
Hamline University, St Paul
Lakewood Community College,
White Bear Lake
Macalester College, St Paul
North Hennepin Community College,
Minneapolis
University of Wisconsin,
River Falls (WI)

Winona State University, Winona

Cross-Enrollments
College of Saint Teresa, Winona
Rochester Community College,
Rochester

Mississippi

Alcorn State University, Lorman

Cross-Enrollment
Copiah-Lincoln Junior College, Wesson

Delta State University, Cleveland

Cross-Enrollment
Mississippi Valley State University,
Itta Bena

Jackson State University, Jackson

Cross-Enrollments
Hinds Junior College, Raymond
Tougaloo College, Tougaloo

Mississippi State University,
Mississippi State

Cross-Enrollments
East Central Junior College, Decatur
East Mississippi Junior College, Scooba

HOST COLLEGES	CROSS-ENROLLMENTS AND EXTENSIONS

Mississippi (continued)

	Extension Meridian Junior College, Meridian
University of Mississippi, University	**Cross-Enrollments** Northeast Mississippi Junior College, Booneville Rust College, Holly Springs
University of Southern Mississippi, Hattiesburg	**Cross-Enrollments** Jones County Junior College, Ellisville Mississippi Gulf Coast Junior College, Gautier Mississippi Gulf Coast Junior College, Perkinston Pearl River Junior College, Poplarville William Carey College, Hattiesburg **Extensions** Copiah-Lincoln Junior College, Wesson Mississippi Gulf Coast Junior College, Gulfport Southwest Mississippi Junior College, Summit

Missouri

Central Missouri State University, Warrensburg	
Kemper Military School and College, Boonville	**Cross-Enrollment** Central Methodist College, Fayette
Lincoln University, Jefferson City	
Missouri Western State College, St Joseph	**Cross-Enrollment** University of Missouri, Kansas City
Northeast Missouri State University, Kirksville	
Northwest Missouri State University, Maryville	

HOST COLLEGES	CROSS-ENROLLMENTS AND EXTENSIONS

Missouri (continued)

Southwest Missouri State University, Springfield	**Cross-Enrollment** Drury College, Springfield **Extensions** Evangel College, Springfield Missouri Southern State College, Joplin
University of Missouri, Columbia	**Cross-Enrollments** Columbia College, Columbia Stephens College, Columbia
University of Missouri, Rolla	
Washington University, St Louis	**Cross-Enrollments** Harris Stowe State College, St Louis St Louis Community College at Florissant Valley, St Louis St Louis Community College at Meramec, Kirkwood Saint Louis University, St Louis Southern Illinois University, Edwardsville (IL) **Extension** University of Missouri, St Louis
Wentworth Military Academy and Junior College, Lexington	
Westminster College, Fulton	**Cross-Enrollment** William Woods College, Fulton

Montana

Montana State University, Bozeman	**Cross-Enrollment** Montana College of Mineral Science and Technology, Butte **Extension** Eastern Montana College, Billings
University of Montana, Missoula	

Nebraska

Creighton University, Omaha	**Cross-Enrollments** Bellevue College, Bellevue College of Saint Mary, Omaha

HOST COLLEGES	CROSS-ENROLLMENTS AND EXTENSIONS

Nebraska (continued)

	Cross-Enrollments Iowa Western Community College, Council Bluffs (IA) Metropolitan Technical Community College, Omaha Peru State College, Peru **Extension** University of Nebraska, Omaha
Kearney State College, Kearney	
University of Nebraska, Lincoln	**Cross-Enrollments** Concordia Teachers College, Seward Doane College, Crete

Nevada

University of Nevada, Las Vegas	
University of Nevada, Reno	

New Hampshire

University of New Hampshire, Durham	**Cross-Enrollments** Keene State College, Keene New England College, Henniker New Hampshire College, Manchester Plymouth State College, Plymouth Rivier College, Nashua Saint Anselm College, Manchester

New Jersey

Princeton University, Princeton	
Rider College, Lawrenceville	**Cross-Enrollments** Burlington County College, Pemberton Mercer County Community College, West Windsor Stockton State College, Pomona Trenton State College, Trenton
Rutgers University, New Brunswick	
Saint Peter's College, Jersey City	**Cross-Enrollments** Columbia University, New York (NY)

HOST COLLEGES	CROSS-ENROLLMENTS AND EXTENSIONS

New Jersey (continued)

Cross-Enrollments
Dominican College of Blauvelt,
    Orangeburg (NY)
Rutgers University, Newark
St Thomas Aquinas College,
    Sparkill (NY)
Stevens Institute of Technology,
    Hoboken
Extensions
Jersey City State College, Jersey City
Monmouth College, West Long Branch

Seton Hall University, South Orange

Cross-Enrollments
Bloomfield College, Bloomfield
Caldwell College, Caldwell
County College of Morris, Randolph
Drew University, Madison
Essex County College, Newark
Fairleigh Dickinson University,
    Madison
Fairleigh Dickinson University,
    Rutherford
Fairleigh Dickinson University,
    Teaneck
Kean College of New Jersey, Union
Montclair State College,
    Upper Montclair
New Jersey Institute of Technology,
    Newark
Passaic County Community College,
    Paterson
Ramapo College of New Jersey,
    Mahwah
Rutgers University, Newark
Union County College, Cranford
Upsala College, East Orange
William Paterson College of New Jersey,
    Wayne

New Mexico

Eastern New Mexico University,
   Portales

Cross-Enrollment
New Mexico Highlands University,
    Las Vegas

HOST COLLEGES	CROSS-ENROLLMENTS AND EXTENSIONS

New Mexico (continued)

	Extension University of Albuquerque, Albuquerque
New Mexico Military Institute, Roswell	
New Mexico State University, Las Cruces	

New York

Canisius College, Buffalo	Cross-Enrollments D'Youville College, Buffalo Erie Community College, Buffalo SUNY, Buffalo SUNY College, Buffalo
Clarkson University, Potsdam	Cross-Enrollment SUNY College, Potsdam

Cornell University, Ithaca	Cross-Enrollments
	Broome Community College,
	    Binghamton
	Corning Community College, Corning
	Ithaca College, Ithaca
	SUNY, Binghamton
	Tompkins Cortland Community
	    College, Dryden
	Extension
	SUNY College, Cortland

Fordham University, Bronx	Cross-Enrollments
	Columbia University, New York
	CUNY Borough of Manhattan
	    Community College, New York
	CUNY City College, New York
	CUNY Herbert H Lehman College,
	    Bronx
	Marist College, Poughkeepsie
	Mount Saint Mary College, Newburgh
	SUNY College, New Paltz
	SUNY College, Purchase
	Extension
	CUNY John Jay College of Criminal
	    Justice, New York

HOST COLLEGES

**CROSS-ENROLLMENTS
AND EXTENSIONS**

New York (continued)

Cross-Enrollments

Hofstra University, Hempstead

Adelphi University, Garden City
Dowling College, Oakdale
Long Island University C W Post
 Campus, Greenvale
Long Island University, Southhampton
Nassau Community College,
 Garden City
New York Institute of Technology,
 Old Westbury
Suffolk County Community College,
 Riverhead
SUNY A&T College, Farmingdale
SUNY College, Old Westbury
SUNY, Stony Brook

Cross-Enrollment

Niagara University, Niagara University

Niagara County Community College,
 Sanborn

Cross-Enrollments

Polytechnic Institute of New York,
 Brooklyn

Columbia University, New York
CUNY Bernard M Baruch College,
 New York
CUNY Brooklyn College, Brooklyn
CUNY City College, New York
CUNY College of Staten Island,
 Staten Island
CUNY Hunter College, New York
CUNY Kingsborough Community
 College, Brooklyn
CUNY Medgar Evers College, Brooklyn
Cuny New York City Technical
 College, Brooklyn
CUNY York College, Jamaica
Long Island University, Brooklyn
Manhattan College, Riverdale
New York Institute of Technology,
 Old Westbury
New York University, New York
Pace University, New York
Pratt Institute, Brooklyn

HOST COLLEGES	CROSS-ENROLLMENTS AND EXTENSIONS

New York (continued)

	Cross-Enrollments St Francis College, Brooklyn Suffolk County Community College, Riverhead
Rensselaer Polytechnic Institute, Troy	**Cross-Enrollments** College of Saint Rose, Albany Hudson Valley Community College, Troy Russell Sage College, Troy SUNY, Albany
Rochester Institute of Technology, Rochester	**Cross-Enrollments** Monroe Community College, Rochester Nazareth College of Rochester, Rochester Roberts Wesleyan College, Rochester St John Fisher College, Rochester SUNY College, Geneseo University of Rochester, Rochester
St Bonaventure University, St Bonaventure	**Cross-Enrollments** Alfred University, Alfred Houghton College, Houghton University of Pittsburgh, Bradford (PA)
St John's University, Jamaica	**Cross-Enrollments** CUNY Borough of Manhattan Community College, New York CUNY Brooklyn College, Brooklyn CUNY City College, New York CUNY College of Staten Island, Staten Island CUNY Fiorello H LaGuardia Community College, Long Island City CUNY New York City Technical College, Brooklyn CUNY Queensborough Community College, Bayside CUNY Queens College, Flushing CUNY York College, Jamaica New York Institute of Technology, Old Westbury

HOST COLLEGES	CROSS-ENROLLMENTS AND EXTENSIONS

New York (continued)

	Cross-Enrollments New York University, New York Wagner College, Staten Island
St Lawrence University, Canton	**Cross-Enrollment** SUNY A&T College, Canton
Siena College, Loudonville	**Cross-Enrollments** Hudson Valley Community College, Troy Schenectady County Community College, Schenectady SUNY, Albany Union College, Schenectady
SUNY College, Brockport	
SUNY College, Fredonia	**Cross-Enrollment** Jamestown Community College, Jamestown
Syracuse University, Syracuse	**Cross-Enrollments** Cayuga County Community College, Auburn Hamilton College, Clinton Le Moyne College, Syracuse Mohawk Valley Community College, Utica Onondaga Community College, Syracuse SUNY College of Environmental Science and Forestry, Syracuse SUNY College of Technology, Utica Utica College of Syracuse University, Utica **Extension** SUNY College, Oswego

North Carolina

Appalachian State University, Boone	**Cross-Enrollment** Lees-McRae College, Banner Elk
Campbell University, Buies Creek	**Cross-Enrollments** Methodist College, Fayetteville Pembroke State University, Pembroke

HOST COLLEGES	CROSS-ENROLLMENTS AND EXTENSIONS
North Carolina (continued)	
	Extension University of North Carolina, Wilmington
Davidson College, Davidson	**Cross-Enrollments** Barber-Scotia College, Concord Belmont Abbey College, Belmont Catawba College, Salisbury Central Piedmont Community College, Charlotte Johnson C Smith University, Charlotte Livingstone College, Salisbury Pfeiffer College, Misenheimer Wingate College, Wingate Winthrop College, Rock Hill (SC) **Extension** University of North Carolina, Charlotte
Duke University, Durham	**Cross-Enrollments** North Carolina Central University, Durham University of North Carolina, Chapel Hill
North Carolina A&T State University, Greensboro	**Cross-Enrollments** Bennett College, Greensboro Greensboro College, Greensboro Guilford College, Greensboro Guilford Technical Community College, Jamestown University of North Carolina, Greensboro **Extension** Elon College, Elon College
North Carolina State University, Raleigh	**Extension** East Carolina University, Greenville
Saint Augustine's College, Raleigh	**Cross-Enrollment** Shaw University, Raleigh **Extension** Elizabeth City State University, Elizabeth City

HOST COLLEGES	CROSS-ENROLLMENTS AND EXTENSIONS

North Carolina (continued)

	Cross-Enrollments
Wake Forest University, Winston-Salem	High Point College, High Point
	Winston-Salem State University, Winston-Salem

Western Carolina University, Cullowhee

North Dakota

	Cross-Enrollments
North Dakota State University, Fargo	Concordia College, Moorhead (MN)
	Moorhead State University, Moorhead (MN)

University of North Dakota, Grand Forks

Ohio

	Cross-Enrollment
Bowling Green State University, Bowling Green	Ohio Northern University, Ada

	Cross-Enrollments
Central State University, Wilberforce	Cedarville College, Cedarville
	Wilberforce University, Wilberforce

	Cross-Enrollments
John Carroll University, University Heights	Case Western Reserve University, Cleveland
	Cleveland State University, Cleveland
	Ursuline College, Pepper Pike

Kent State University, Kent

	Cross-Enrollments
Ohio State University, Columbus	Capital University, Columbus
	Columbus Technical Institute, Columbus
	Denison University, Granville
	DeVry Institute of Technology, Columbus
	Ohio Dominican College, Columbus
	Ohio Wesleyan University, Delaware
	Otterbein College, Westerville
	Extension
	Franklin University, Columbus

HOST COLLEGES	CROSS-ENROLLMENTS AND EXTENSIONS

Ohio (continued)

Ohio University, Athens	**Extension** Rio Grande College/Community College, Rio Grande
University of Akron, Akron	
University of Cincinnati, Cincinnati	
University of Dayton, Dayton	**Cross-Enrollment** Sinclair Community College, Dayton **Extension** Wright State University, Dayton
University of Toledo, Toledo	
Xavier University, Cincinnati	**Cross-Enrollment** Miami University, Oxford **Extension** Northern Kentucky University, Highland Heights (KY)
Youngstown State University, Youngstown	

Oklahoma

Cameron University, Lawton	
Central State University, Edmond	**Cross-Enrollment** Langston University, Langston
East Central Oklahoma State University, Ada	**Cross-Enrollment** Southeastern Oklahoma State University, Durant
Northwestern Oklahoma State University, Alva	**Extension** Oklahoma Panhandle State University, Goodwell
Oklahoma State University, Stillwater	**Cross-Enrollment** Rogers State College, Claremore **Extension** University of Tulsa, Tulsa
Southwestern Oklahoma State University, Weatherford	
University of Oklahoma, Norman	

HOST COLLEGES

CROSS-ENROLLMENTS AND EXTENSIONS

Oregon

	Extension
Oregon State University, Corvallis	Portland State University, Portland
	Extension
University of Oregon, Eugene	Oregon Institute of Technology, Klamath Falls

Pennsylvania

	Cross-Enrollments
Bucknell University, Lewisburg	Bloomsburg University of Pennsylvania, Bloomsburg
	Lycoming College, Williamsport
	Susquehanna University, Selinsgrove
	Extension
	Mansfield University of Pennsylvania, Mansfield
Carnegie-Mellon University, Pittsburgh	
Clarion University of Pennsylvania, Clarion	
	Cross-Enrollments
Dickinson College, Carlisle	Harrisburg Area Community College, Harrisburg
	Lebanon Valley College, Annville
	Pennsylvania State University, Middletown
Drexel University, Philadelphia	
	Cross-Enrollments
Duquesne University, Pittsburgh	Allegheny College, Meadville
	Community College of Allegheny County, Pittsburgh
	Point Park College, Pittsburgh
	Robert Morris College, Coraopolis
	Cross-Enrollments
Gannon University, Erie	Allegheny College, Meadville
	Edinboro University of Pennsylvania, Edinboro
	Jamestown Community College, Jamestown (NY)

HOST COLLEGES	CROSS-ENROLLMENTS AND EXTENSIONS

Pennsylvania (continued)

	Cross-Enrollments Mercyhurst College, Erie Villa Maria College, Erie
Gettysburg College, Gettysburg	**Cross-Enrollment** York College of Pennsylvania, York **Extensions** Millersville University of Pennsylvania, Millersville Mount Saint Mary's College, Emmitsburg (MD)
Indiana University of Pennsylvania, Indiana	**Cross-Enrollments** Saint Francis College, Loretto Saint Vincent College, Latrobe West Chester University of Pennsylvania, West Chester **Extension** Slippery Rock University of Pennsylvania, Slippery Rock
Lafayette College, Easton	**Extension** East Stroudsburg University of Pennsylvania, East Stroudsburg
La Salle University, Philadelphia	**Cross-Enrollments** Community College, Philadelphia Philadelphia College of Textiles and Science, Philadelphia Saint Joseph's University, Philadelphia Spring Garden College, Philadelphia
Lehigh University, Bethlehem	**Cross-Enrollments** Albright College, Reading Allentown College of St Francis de Sales, Center Valley Cedar Crest College, Allentown Kutztown University of Pennsylvania, Kutztown Lehigh County Community College, Schnecksville Moravian College, Bethlehem Muhlenberg College, Allentown

HOST COLLEGES

CROSS-ENROLLMENTS AND EXTENSIONS

Pennsylvania (continued)

Pennsylvania State University, University Park	**Cross-Enrollment** Pennsylvania State University—Berks Campus, Reading **Extensions** Lock Haven University of Pennsylvania, Lock Haven Pennsylvania State University, Altoona Pennsylvania State University—Behrend College, Erie Pennsylvania State University—Delaware County Campus, Media Pennsylvania State University, Hazelton Pennsylvania State University—Ogontz Campus, Abington Pennsylvania State University, Schuylkill Haven
Shippensburg University of Pennsylvania, Shippensburg	**Cross-Enrollment** Pennsylvania State University, Mont Alto
Temple University, Philadelphia	
University of Pennsylvania, Philadelphia	**Cross-Enrollments** Glassboro State College, Glassboro (NJ) Philadelphia College of Pharmacy and Science, Philadelphia Rutgers University, Camden (NJ) Villanova University, Villanova
University of Pittsburgh, Pittsburgh	**Cross-Enrollments** Butler County Community College, Butler Carlow College, Pittsburgh Community College of Allegheny County—Boyce Campus, Monroeville Community College of Allegheny County, Pittsburgh University of Pittsburgh, Greensburg

HOST COLLEGES	CROSS-ENROLLMENTS AND EXTENSIONS

Pennsylvania (continued)

University of Scranton, Scranton	**Cross-Enrollments** Baptist Bible College of Pennsylvania, Clarks Summit College Misericordia, Dallas Keystone Junior College, La Plume King's College, Wilkes-Barre Lackawanna Junior College, Scranton Luzerne County Community College, Nanticoke Marywood College, Scranton Pennsylvania State University, Wilkes-Barre Pennsylvania State University— Worthington Scranton Campus, Dunmore Wilkes College, Wilkes-Barre
Valley Forge Military Junior College, Wayne	**Cross-Enrollment** Eastern College, St Davids
Washington and Jefferson College, Washington	**Extension** California University of Pennsylvania, California
Widener University, Chester	**Cross-Enrollments** Cheyney University of Pennsylvania, Cheyney Villanova University, Villanova West Chester University of Pennsylvania, West Chester

Puerto Rico

University of Puerto Rico, Mayagüez	**Cross-Enrollments** American College of Puerto Rico, Bayamón Catholic University of Puerto Rico, Ponce Electronic Data Processing College of Puerto Rico, Hato Rey Inter American University of Puerto Rico, Aguadilla

HOST COLLEGES	CROSS-ENROLLMENTS AND EXTENSIONS

Puerto Rico (continued)

Cross-Enrollments
Inter American University of
  Puerto Rico, Arecibo
Inter American University of
  Puerto Rico, Ponce
Inter American University of
  Puerto Rico, San Germán
International Institute of the Americas
  of World University, Hato Rey

Cross-Enrollments

University of Puerto Rico, Río Piedras

American College of Puerto Rico,
  Bayamón
Bayamón Central University, Bayamón
Caribbean University College, Bayamón
Colegio Universitario Metropolitano,
  Cupey
Electronic Data Processing College of
  Puerto Rico, Hato Rey
Instituto Comercial de Puerto Rico
  Junior College, Hato Rey
Inter American University of
  Puerto Rico, Fajardo
Inter American University of
  Puerto Rico, Guayama
Inter American University of
  Puerto Rico, Hato Rey
International Institute of the Americas
  of World University, Hato Rey
Puerto Rico Junior College,
  Río Piedras
Universidad del Turabo, Caguas
Universidad Polytécnica de
  Puerto Rico, Hato Rey
University of Puerto Rico, Cayey
University of Puerto Rico, Humacao
University of Puerto Rico Medical
  Sciences Campus, San Juan
University of Puerto Rico, Río Piedras
University of the Sacred Heart,
  Santurce

HOST COLLEGES	CROSS-ENROLLMENTS AND EXTENSIONS

Rhode Island

Providence College, Providence	**Cross-Enrollments**
	Barrington College, Barrington
	Bristol Community College,
	    Fall River (MA)
	Brown University, Providence
	Community College of Rhode Island,
	    Warwick
	Johnson & Wales College, Providence
	Roger Williams College, Bristol
	Salve Regina–The Newport College,
	    Newport
	Southeastern Massachusetts University,
	    North Dartmouth (MA)
	Extensions
	Bryant College, Smithfield
	Rhode Island College, Providence

University of Rhode Island, Kingston	

South Carolina

The Citadel, Charleston (men only)	
Clemson University, Clemson	**Cross-Enrollments** Anderson College, Anderson Central Wesleyan College, Central Tri-County Technical College, Pendleton
Furman University, Greenville	**Cross-Enrollment** Greenville Technical College, Greenville **Extension** Benedict College, Columbia
Presbyterian College, Clinton	**Cross-Enrollments** Lander College, Greenwood Newberry College, Newberry
South Carolina State College, Orangeburg	**Cross-Enrollments** Claflin College, Orangeburg Voorhees College, Denmark

University of South Carolina,
    Columbia
	Cross-Enrollment
	University of South Carolina–
	    Coastal Carolina College, Conway

HOST COLLEGES	CROSS-ENROLLMENTS AND EXTENSIONS

South Carolina (continued)

	Extension Francis Marion College, Florence
Wofford College, Spartanburg	**Cross-Enrollments** Converse College, Spartanburg Spartanburg Methodist College, Spartanburg University of South Carolina, Spartanburg **Extension** Erskine College, Due West

South Dakota

South Dakota School of Mines and Technology, Rapid City	**Cross-Enrollment** National College, Rapid City **Extension** Black Hills State College, Spearfish
South Dakota State University, Brookings	**Cross-Enrollment** Dakota State College, Madison **Extension** Northern State College, Aberdeen
University of South Dakota, Vermillion	**Cross-Enrollments** Dordt College, Sioux Center (IA) Mount Marty College, Yankton Yankton College, Yankton

Tennessee

Austin Peay State University, Clarksville	
Carson-Newman College, Jefferson City	**Cross-Enrollments** Lincoln Memorial University, Harrogate Morristown College, Morristown
East Tennessee State University, Johnson City	**Cross-Enrollments** Milligan College, Milligan College Tusculum College, Greeneville
Memphis State University, Memphis	**Cross-Enrollments** Christian Brothers College, Memphis LeMoyne-Owen College, Memphis

HOST COLLEGES	CROSS-ENROLLMENTS AND EXTENSIONS

Tennessee (continued)

	Cross-Enrollments Rhodes College, Memphis Shelby State Community College, Memphis
Middle Tennessee State University, Murfreesboro	
Tennessee Technological University, Cookeville	
University of Tennessee, Chattanooga	**Cross-Enrollment** Bryan College, Dayton
University of Tennessee, Knoxville	**Cross-Enrollment** Knoxville College, Knoxville
University of Tennessee, Martin	
Vanderbilt University, Nashville	**Cross-Enrollments** Aquinas Junior College, Nashville Belmont College, Nashville David Lipscomb College, Nashville Fisk University, Nashville Tennessee State University, Nashville Trevecca Nazarene College, Nashville

Texas

Bishop College, Dallas	**Cross-Enrollments** Dallas Baptist University, Dallas Jarvis Christian College, Hawkins **Extension** Texas College, Tyler
Hardin-Simmons University, Abilene	**Cross-Enrollments** Abilene Christian University, Abilene McMurry College, Abilene **Extension** Howard Payne University, Brownwood
Midwestern State University, Wichita Falls	
Pan American University, Edinburg	**Cross-Enrollment** Texas Southmost College, Brownsville
Prairie View A&M University, Prairie View	

HOST COLLEGES	CROSS-ENROLLMENTS AND EXTENSIONS

Texas (continued)

Rice University, Houston	**Cross-Enrollment** Houston Baptist University, Houston
St Mary's University of San Antonio, San Antonio	**Cross-Enrollments** Our Lady of the Lake University of San Antonio, San Antonio San Antonio College, San Antonio
Sam Houston State University, Huntsville	
Stephen F Austin State University, Nacogdoches	
Texas A&I University, Kingsville	**Cross-Enrollment** Corpus Christi State University, Corpus Christi
Texas A&M University, College Station	**Extension** Tarleton State University, Stephenville
Texas Christian University, Fort Worth	**Cross-Enrollments** Tarrant County Junior College, Fort Worth Texas Wesleyan College, Fort Worth
Texas Tech University, Lubbock	
Trinity University, San Antonio	**Cross-Enrollments** Incarnate Word College, San Antonio St Philip's College, San Antonio San Antonio College, San Antonio
University of Houston, Houston	**Cross-Enrollment** Texas Southern University, Houston
University of Texas, Arlington	**Extension** Texas Woman's University, Denton
University of Texas, Austin	**Cross-Enrollments** Austin Community College, Austin Huston-Tillotson College, Austin Southwest Texas State University, San Marcos
University of Texas, El Paso	
University of Texas, San Antonio	**Cross-Enrollment** San Antonio College, San Antonio
West Texas State University, Canyon	

HOST COLLEGES	CROSS-ENROLLMENTS AND EXTENSIONS

Utah

Brigham Young University, Provo	**Cross-Enrollment** Utah Technical College, Provo
University of Utah, Salt Lake City	
Utah State University, Logan	
Weber State College, Ogden	

Vermont

Norwich University, The Military College of Vermont, Northfield	**Cross-Enrollment** Dartmouth College, Hanover (NH)
University of Vermont, Burlington	**Cross-Enrollments** Castleton State College, Castleton Champlain College, Burlington Johnson State College, Johnson Middlebury College, Middlebury Saint Michael's College, Winooski

Virginia

College of William and Mary, Williamsburg	**Extension** Christopher Newport College, Newport News
Hampton University, Hampton	**Cross-Enrollment** Thomas Nelson Community College, Hampton
James Madison University, Harrisonburg	**Cross-Enrollment** Blue Ridge Community College, Weyers Cave
Norfolk State University, Norfolk	
Old Dominion University, Norfolk	**Cross-Enrollment** Tidewater Community College, Virginia Beach
University of Richmond, Richmond	**Cross-Enrollments** Hampden-Sydney College, Hampden-Sydney Randolph-Macon College, Ashland Virginia Commonwealth University, Richmond

HOST COLLEGES

CROSS-ENROLLMENTS
AND EXTENSIONS

Virginia (continued)

	Extension Longwood College, Farmville
University of Virginia, Charlottesville	**Cross-Enrollment** Piedmont Virginia Community College, Charlottesville
Virginia Military Institute, Lexington (men only)	
Virginia Polytechnic Institute and State University, Blacksburg	**Cross-Enrollments** Ferrum College, Ferrum Radford University, Radford
Virginia State University, Petersburg	**Cross-Enrollments** John Tyler Community College, Chester Richard Bland College, Petersburg Saint Paul's College, Lawrenceville Virginia Union University, Richmond
Washington and Lee University, Lexington	**Cross-Enrollments** Central Virginia Community College, Lynchburg Liberty University, Lynchburg Randolph-Macon Woman's College, Lynchburg Sweet Briar College, Sweet Briar **Extension** Lynchburg College, Lynchburg

Washington

Eastern Washington University, Cheney	**Extension** Central Washington University, Ellensburg
Gonzaga University, Spokane	**Cross-Enrollments** Spokane Community College, Spokane Spokane Falls Community College, Spokane Whitworth College, Spokane
Seattle University, Seattle	**Cross-Enrollments** Fort Steilacoom Community College, Tacoma

HOST COLLEGES	CROSS-ENROLLMENTS AND EXTENSIONS
Washington (continued)	
	Cross-Enrollments Pacific Lutheran University, Tacoma Saint Martin's College, Lacey Seattle Pacific University, Seattle Tacoma Community College, Tacoma University of Puget Sound, Tacoma
University of Washington, Seattle	**Cross-Enrollments** Bellevue Community College, Bellevue Everett Community College, Everett Seattle Pacific University, Seattle
Washington State University, Pullman	**Cross-Enrollment** North Seattle Community College, Seattle **Extension** Eastern Oregon State College, La Grande (OR)
West Virginia	
Marshall University, Huntington	
West Virginia State College, Institute	**Cross-Enrollments** University of Charleston, Charleston West Virginia Institute of Technology, Montgomery
West Virginia University, Morgantown	**Cross-Enrollment** Fairmont State College, Fairmont **Extension** Frostburg State College, Frostburg (MD)
Wisconsin	
Marquette University, Milwaukee	**Cross-Enrollment** University of Wisconsin–Parkside, Kenosha
Ripon College, Ripon	**Cross-Enrollment** Marian College of Fond du Lac, Fond du Lac
St Norbert College, De Pere	**Cross-Enrollment** University of Wisconsin, Green Bay

HOST COLLEGES

CROSS-ENROLLMENTS
AND EXTENSIONS

Wisconsin (continued)

	Cross-Enrollment
University of Wisconsin, La Crosse	Viterbo College, La Crosse
University of Wisconsin, Madison	
	Cross-Enrollments
University of Wisconsin, Milwaukee	Cardinal Stritch College, Milwaukee
	University of Wisconsin Centers
	(13 locations)
University of Wisconsin, Oshkosh	
	Cross-Enrollment
University of Wisconsin, Platteville	University of Dubuque, Dubuque (IA)
University of Wisconsin, Stevens Point	
University of Wisconsin, Whitewater	

Wyoming

University of Wyoming, Laramie

Navy ROTC Programs

HOST COLLEGES	CROSS-ENROLLMENTS
Alabama	
Auburn University, Auburn University	
Arizona	
University of Arizona, Tucson	
California	
San Diego State University, San Diego	University of California, La Jolla
University of California, Berkeley	California State University, Hayward
	California State University, Sacramento
	San Francisco State University, San Francisco
	San Jose State University, San Jose
	Stanford University, Stanford
	University of California, Davis
	University of San Francisco, San Francisco
	University of Santa Clara, Santa Clara
University of California, Los Angeles	California State University, Fullerton
	California State University, Long Beach
	California State University, Los Angeles
	California State University, Northridge
	Loyola Marymount University, Los Angeles
	Northrop University, Inglewood
	Occidental College, Los Angeles

HOST COLLEGES	CROSS-ENROLLMENTS
California (continued)	
	Pepperdine University, Malibu University of California, Irvine
University of San Diego, San Diego	University of California, La Jolla

University of Southern California,
  Los Angeles
	California Institute of Technology,
	  Pasadena
	California State Polytechnic University,
	  Pomona
	Claremont McKenna College,
	  Claremont
	Harvey Mudd College, Claremont

Colorado

University of Colorado, Boulder	

District of Columbia

George Washington University,
  Washington
	American University, Washington
	Catholic University of America,
	  Washington
	Georgetown University, Washington
	Howard University, Washington
	University of Maryland,
	  College Park (MD)
	University of the District of Columbia,
	  Washington

Florida

Florida A&M University, Tallahassee	Florida State University, Tallahassee Tallahassee Community College, Tallahassee
Jacksonville University, Jacksonville	Edward Waters College, Jacksonville Florida Junior College, Jacksonville University of North Florida, Jacksonville
University of Florida, Gainesville	

Georgia

Georgia Institute of Technology, Atlanta	Agnes Scott College, Decatur Clark College, Atlanta Georgia State University, Atlanta

HOST COLLEGES	CROSS-ENROLLMENTS

Georgia (continued)

	Kennesaw College, Marietta
	Morehouse College, Atlanta
	Morris Brown College, Atlanta
	Oglethorpe University, Atlanta
	Southern Technical Institute, Marietta
	Spelman College, Atlanta
Savannah State College, Savannah	Armstrong State College, Savannah

Idaho

University of Idaho, Moscow	Washington State University, Pullman (WA)

Illinois

Illinois Institute of Technology, Chicago	City Colleges of Chicago, Wilbur Wright College, Chicago
	Elmhurst College, Elmhurst
	Prairie State College, Chicago Heights
	Purdue University Calumet, Hammond (IN)
	University of Chicago, Chicago
	University of Illinois, Chicago
Northwestern University, Evanston	Loyola University of Chicago, Chicago
University of Illinois, Urbana	Parkland College, Champaign

Indiana

Purdue University, West Lafayette	
University of Notre Dame, Notre Dame	Bethel College, Mishawaka
	Indiana University, South Bend
	Saint Mary's College, Notre Dame

Iowa

Iowa State University, Ames	

Kansas

University of Kansas, Lawrence	

Louisiana

Southern University and A&M College, Baton Rouge	Louisiana State University and A&M College, Baton Rouge

HOST COLLEGES	CROSS-ENROLLMENTS
Louisiana (continued)	
Tulane University, New Orleans	

Maine

Maine Maritime Academy, Castine*	University of Maine, Orono

Massachusetts

Boston University, Boston	Northeastern University, Boston
College of the Holy Cross, Worcester	Anna Maria College, Paxton Assumption College, Worcester Central New England College, Worcester Clark University, Worcester Worcester Polytechnic Institute, Worcester Worcester State College, Worcester
Massachusetts Institute of Technology, Cambridge	Harvard University, Cambridge Tufts University, Medford Wellesley College, Wellesley

Michigan

University of Michigan, Ann Arbor	Eastern Michigan University, Ypsilanti

Minnesota

University of Minnesota, Minneapolis	Augsburg College, Minneapolis College of St Thomas, St Paul Macalester College, St Paul

Mississippi

University of Mississippi, University	

Missouri

University of Missouri, Columbia	Columbia College, Columbia

Nebraska

University of Nebraska, Lincoln	Nebraska Wesleyan University, Lincoln

*Marine Corps option not available.

HOST COLLEGES	CROSS-ENROLLMENTS
New Mexico	•
University of New Mexico, Albuquerque	University of Albuquerque, Albuquerque
New York	
Cornell University, Ithaca	Ithaca College, Ithaca SUNY College, Cortland
Rensselaer Polytechnic Institute, Troy	Russell Sage College, Troy Siena College, Loudonville Skidmore College, Saratoga Springs SUNY, Albany Union College, Schenectady
SUNY Maritime College, Bronx*	Fordham University, Bronx Iona College, New Rochelle Manhattan College, Riverdale
University of Rochester, Rochester	Monroe Community College, Rochester Nazareth College, Rochester Rochester Institute of Technology, Rochester St John Fisher College, Rochester SUNY College, Brockport SUNY College, Geneseo
North Carolina	
Duke University, Durham	North Carolina Central University, Durham
University of North Carolina, Chapel Hill	North Carolina State University, Raleigh
Ohio	
Miami University, Oxford	
Ohio State University, Columbus	Capital University, Columbus Ohio Dominican College, Columbus Otterbein College, Westerville
Oklahoma	
University of Oklahoma, Norman	

*Marine Corps option not available.

HOST COLLEGES	CROSS-ENROLLMENTS

Oregon

Oregon State University, Corvallis	Linn-Benton Community College, Albany

Pennsylvania

Pennsylvania State University, University Park	
University of Pennsylvania, Philadelphia	Drexel University, Philadelphia La Salle University, Philadelphia Saint Joseph's University, Philadelphia Temple University, Philadelphia
Villanova University, Villanova	Temple University, Philadelphia

South Carolina

The Citadel, Charleston (men only)	
University of South Carolina, Columbia	

Tennessee

Memphis State University, Memphis	
Vanderbilt University, Nashville	Belmont College, Nashville David Lipscomb College, Nashville Fisk University, Nashville Tennessee State University, Nashville Trevecca Nazarene College, Nashville

Texas

Prairie View A&M University, Prairie View	
Rice University, Houston	Houston Baptist University, Houston Texas Southern University, Houston University of Houston, Houston University of St Thomas, Houston
Texas A&M University, College Station	
Texas Tech University, Lubbock	
University of Texas, Austin	

Utah

University of Utah, Salt Lake City	Weber State College, Ogden Westminster College, Salt Lake City

HOST COLLEGES	CROSS-ENROLLMENTS

Vermont

Norwich University, Northfield

Virginia

Hampton University, Hampton

Norfolk State University, Norfolk

Old Dominion University, Norfolk

University of Virginia, Charlottesville

Virginia Military Institute, Lexington (men only)

Virginia Polytechnic Institute and State University, Blacksburg

Washington

| University of Washington, Seattle | Seattle Pacific University, Seattle
Seattle University, Seattle |

Wisconsin

| Marquette University, Milwaukee | Milwaukee School of Engineering, Milwaukee
Mount Mary College, Milwaukee
University of Wisconsin, Milwaukee |

University of Wisconsin, Madison

Air Force ROTC Programs

HOST COLLEGES	CROSS-ENROLLMENTS
Alabama	
Alabama State University, Montgomery	Auburn University, Montgomery Huntingdon College, Montgomery Troy State University, Montgomery
Auburn University, Auburn University	
Samford University, Birmingham	Birmingham-Southern College, Birmingham Jefferson State Junior College, Birmingham Lawson State Community College, Birmingham Miles College, Birmingham University of Alabama, Birmingham University of Montevallo, Montevallo
Troy State University, Troy	
Tuskegee Institute, Tuskegee Institute	
University of Alabama, University	
Arizona	
Arizona State University, Tempe	Glendale Community College, Glendale Grand Canyon College, Phoenix Mesa Community College, Mesa Phoenix College, Phoenix Scottsdale Community College, Scottsdale South Mountain Community College, Phoenix

HOST COLLEGES	CROSS-ENROLLMENTS

Arizona (continued)

Embry-Riddle Aeronautical University, Prescott	Yavapai College, Prescott
Northern Arizona University, Flagstaff	
University of Arizona, Tucson	Pima Community College, Tucson

Arkansas

University of Arkansas, Fayetteville	

California

California State University, Fresno	College of the Sequoias, Visalia Fresno City College, Fresno Kings River Community College, Reedley Merced College, Merced West Coast Christian College, Fresno West Hills College, Coalinga
California State University, Long Beach	California State University, San Bernardino California State Polytechnic University, Pomona California State University, Dominguez Hills, Carson California State University, Fullerton California State University, Los Angeles Chaffey College, Alta Loma Citrus College, Azusa Cypress College, Cypress El Camino College, Torrance Fullerton College, Fullerton Golden West College, Huntington Beach Long Beach City College, Long Beach Los Angeles Harbor College, Wilmington Mt San Jacinto College, San Jacinto Orange Coast College, Costa Mesa Pasadena City College, Pasadena Rio Hondo Community College, Whittier

HOST COLLEGES

California (continued)

CROSS-ENROLLMENTS

Riverside City College, Riverside
Saddleback Community College,
  Mission Viejo
San Bernardino Valley College,
  San Bernardino
Santa Ana College, Santa Ana
University of California, Riverside

California State University, Sacramento — American River College, Sacramento
Butte College, Oroville
Cosumnes River College, Sacramento
Sacramento City College, Sacramento
Sierra College, Rocklin
Solano Community College,
  Suisun City
University of California, Davis
University of the Pacific, Stockton
Yuba College, Marysville

Loyola Marymount University,
  Los Angeles

Antelope Valley College, Lancaster
California State Polytechnic
  University, Pomona
California State University,
  Dominguez Hills, Carson
California State University, Fullerton
California State University,
  Long Beach
California State University,
  Los Angeles
California State University, Northridge
California State University,
  San Bernardino
Chapman College, Orange
Cypress College, Cypress
East Los Angeles College,
  Monterey Park
El Camino College, Torrance
Fullerton College, Fullerton
Golden West College,
  Huntington Beach
Los Angeles City College, Los Angeles
Los Angeles Harbor College,
  Wilmington

HOST COLLEGES

CROSS-ENROLLMENTS

California (continued)

	Los Angeles Pierce College, Woodland Hills
	Los Angeles Southwest College, Los Angeles
	Los Angeles Trade-Technical College, Los Angeles
	Los Angeles Valley College, Van Nuys
	Marymount Palos Verdes College, Rancho Palos Verdes
	Moorpark College, Moorpark
	Mount St Mary's College, Los Angeles
	Mt San Jacinto College, San Jacinto
	Northrop University, Inglewood
	Orange Coast College, Costa Mesa
	Pasadena City College, Pasadena
	Pepperdine University, Malibu
	Rio Hondo Community College, Whittier
	Riverside City College, Riverside
	Saddleback Community College, Mission Viejo
	San Bernardino Valley College, San Bernardino
	Santa Ana College, Santa Ana
	Santa Monica College, Santa Monica
	University of California, Irvine
	University of California, Riverside
	University of Redlands, Redlands
	Victor Valley College, Victorville
	West Los Angeles College, Culver City
	Westmont College, Santa Barbara
San Diego State University, San Diego	Cuyamaca Community College, El Cajon
	Grossmont College, El Cajon
	National University, San Diego
	Palomar College, San Marcos
	Point Loma Nazarene College, San Diego
	San Diego City College, San Diego
	San Diego Mesa College, San Diego
	San Diego Miramar College, San Diego
	Southwestern College, Chula Vista

HOST COLLEGES	CROSS-ENROLLMENTS
California (continued)	
	University of California, La Jolla
	University of San Diego, San Diego
San Francisco State University, San Francisco	Cogswell College, San Francisco
	Dominican College of San Rafael, San Rafael
	Golden Gate University, San Francisco
	University of San Francisco, San Francisco
San Jose State University, San Jose	Cabrillo College, Aptos
	De Anza College, Cupertino
	Evergreen Valley College, San Jose
	Foothill College, Los Altos Hills
	Mission College, Santa Clara
	Ohlone College, Fremont
	San Jose City College, San Jose
	Stanford University, Stanford
	University of Santa Clara, Santa Clara
	West Valley College, Saratoga
University of California, Berkeley	California State University, Hayward
	Chabot College, Hayward
	City College of San Francisco, San Francisco
	College of Alameda, Alameda
	Contra Costa College, San Pablo
	Diablo Valley College, Pleasant Hill
	Graduate Theological Union, Berkeley
	Holy Names College, Oakland
	Laney College, Oakland
	Los Medanos College, Pittsburg
	Merritt College, Oakland
	Mills College, Oakland
	Ohlone College, Fremont
	Saint Mary's College of California, Moraga
	Sonoma State University, Rohnert Park
University of California, Los Angeles	California Lutheran College, Thousand Oaks
	California State College, San Bernardino

HOST COLLEGES	CROSS-ENROLLMENTS

California (continued)

	California State Polytechnic University, Pomona
	California State University, Dominguez Hills, Carson
	California State University, Fullerton
	California State University, Long Beach
	California State University, Los Angeles
	California State University, Northridge
	Los Angeles Mission College, San Fernando
	Mount St. Mary's College, Los Angeles
	Northrop University, Inglewood
	Santa Monica College, Santa Monica
	Southern Illinois University, Sunnymead
	University of California, Irvine
	University of California, Riverside
	University of California, Santa Barbara
	University of La Verne, La Verne

University of Southern California, Los Angeles	Biola University, La Mirada
	California Institute of Technology, Pasadena
	California Lutheran College, Thousand Oaks
	California State College, San Bernardino
	California State Polytechnic University, Pomona
	California State University, Dominguez Hills, Carson
	California State University, Fullerton
	California State University, Los Angeles
	California State University, Northridge
	Chaffey College, Alta Loma
	Chapman College, Orange
	Citrus College, Azusa
	Claremont McKenna College, Claremont
	Compton Community College, Compton

HOST COLLEGES	CROSS-ENROLLMENTS

California (continued)

Cypress College, Cypress
East Los Angeles College,
   Monterey Park
El Camino College, Torrance
Fullerton College, Fullerton
Glendale Community College,
   Glendale
Golden West College,
   Huntington Beach
Harvey Mudd College, Claremont
Long Beach City College,
   Long Beach
Los Angeles City College, Los Angeles
Los Angeles Harbor College,
   Wilmington
Los Angeles Pierce College,
   Woodland Hills
Los Angeles Southwest College,
   Los Angeles
Los Angeles Trade-Technical College,
   Los Angeles
Los Angeles Valley College, Van Nuys
Moorpark College, Moorpark
Mt San Antonio College, Walnut
Northrop University, Inglewood
Occidental College, Los Angeles
Orange Coast College, Costa Mesa
Pasadena City College, Pasadena
Pepperdine University, Malibu
Pomona College, Claremont
Rio Hondo Community College,
   Whittier
San Bernardino Valley College,
   San Bernardino
University of California, Irvine
University of California, Riverside
Ventura College, Ventura
West Los Angeles College, Culver City
Whittier College, Whittier

Colorado

Colorado State University, Fort Collins

HOST COLLEGES	CROSS-ENROLLMENTS

Colorado (continued)

University of Colorado, Boulder	Arapahoe Community College, Littleton Colorado School of Mines, Golden Metropolitan State College, Denver Regis College, Denver University of Colorado, Denver University of Colorado Health Sciences Center, Denver University of Denver, Denver
University of Northern Colorado, Greeley	Aims Community College, Greeley

Connecticut

University of Connecticut, Storrs	Central Connecticut State University, New Britain Eastern Connecticut State University, Willimantic Southern Connecticut State University, New Haven Trinity College, Hartford University of Hartford, West Hartford Western Connecticut State University, Danbury

Delaware

University of Delaware, Newark	Wilmington College, New Castle

District of Columbia

Howard University, Washington	American University, Washington Catholic University of America, Washington Georgetown University, Washington George Washington University, Washington Trinity College, Washington University of the District of Columbia, Washington

Florida

Embry-Riddle Aeronautical University, Daytona Beach	Bethune-Cookman College, Daytona Beach

HOST COLLEGES	CROSS-ENROLLMENTS

Florida (continued)

	Daytona Beach Community College, Daytona Beach
	University of Central Florida, Daytona Center
Florida State University, Tallahassee	Florida A&M University, Tallahassee
	Tallahassee Community College, Tallahassee
University of Central Florida, Orlando	Brevard Community College, Cocoa
	Florida Southern College, Orlando Campus, Orlando
	Lake-Sumter Community College, Leesburg
	Rollins College, Winter Park
	Seminole Community College, Sanford
	Valencia Community College, Orlando
University of Florida, Gainesville	Santa Fe Community College, Gainesville
University of Miami, Coral Gables	Barry University, Miami Shores
	Florida International University, Miami
	Florida Memorial College, Miami
	Miami-Dade Community College, Miami
	St Thomas of Villanova University, Miami
University of South Florida, Tampa	Hillsborough Community College, Tampa
	Pasco-Hernando Community College, Dade City
	Polk Community College, Winter Haven
	Saint Leo College, Saint Leo
	St Petersburg Junior College, St Petersburg
	University of Tampa, Tampa

Georgia

Georgia Institute of Technology, Atlanta	Agnes Scott College, Decatur
	Clark College, Atlanta
	Georgia State University, Atlanta

HOST COLLEGES	CROSS-ENROLLMENTS

Georgia (continued)

	Morehouse College, Atlanta
	Morris Brown College, Atlanta
	Southern Technical Institute, Marietta
	Spelman College, Atlanta
University of Georgia, Athens	Medical College of Georgia, Augusta
Valdosta State College, Valdosta	

Hawaii

University of Hawaii at Manoa, Honolulu	Chaminade University, Honolulu
	Hawaii Pacific College, Honolulu
	Honolulu Community College, Honolulu
	Kapiolani Community College, Honolulu
	Leeward Community College, Pearl City
	West Oahu College, Pearl City
	Windward Community College, Kaneohe

Illinois

Illinois Institute of Technology, Chicago	Chicago State University, Chicago
	Elmhurst College, Elmhurst
	Governors State University, University Park
	Harry S Truman College, Chicago
	John Marshall Law School, Chicago
	Kennedy-King College, Chicago
	Lewis University, Romeoville
	Loop College, Chicago
	Malcolm X College, Chicago
	North Central College, Naperville
	Northeastern Illinois University, Chicago
	Northern Illinois University, De Kalb
	Northwestern University, Evanston
	Olive-Harvey College, Chicago
	Richard J Daley College, Chicago
	Rush University, Chicago
	Saint Xavier College, Chicago
	Triton College, River Grove

HOST COLLEGES	CROSS-ENROLLMENTS
Illinois (continued)	
	University of Illinois, Chicago Wilbur Wright College, Chicago
Parks College of Saint Louis University, Cahokia	Harris Stowe State College, St Louis (MO) St Louis Community Colleges, St Louis (MO) Saint Louis University, St Louis (MO) University of Missouri, St Louis (MO) Washington University, St Louis (MO)
Southern Illinois University, Carbondale	John A Logan College, Carterville
Southern Illinois University, Edwardsville	Belleville Area College, Belleville Lewis and Clark Community College, Godfrey McKendree College, Lebanon
University of Illinois, Urbana	Parkland College, Champaign
Indiana	
Indiana University, Bloomington	Butler University, Indianapolis DePauw University, Greencastle Indiana State University, Terre Haute Indiana University–Purdue University, Indianapolis Marian College, Indianapolis Rose-Hulman Institute of Technology, Terre Haute
Purdue University, West Lafayette	
University of Notre Dame, Notre Dame	Holy Cross Junior College, Notre Dame Indiana University, South Bend Saint Mary's College, Notre Dame
Iowa	
Iowa State University, Ames	Drake University, Des Moines
University of Iowa, Iowa City	
Kansas	
Kansas State University, Manhattan	

HOST COLLEGES	CROSS-ENROLLMENTS

Kansas (continued)

| University of Kansas, Lawrence | Mid-America Nazarene College, Olathe
Washburn University, Topeka |

Kentucky

University of Kentucky, Lexington	Eastern Kentucky University, Richmond Georgetown College, Georgetown Kentucky State University, Frankfort Midway College, Midway Transylvania University, Lexington
University of Louisville, Louisville	Bellarmine College, Louisville Indiana University Southeast, New Albany (IN) Louisville Presbyterian Theological Seminary, Louisville Southern Baptist Theological Seminary, Louisville Spalding University, Louisville

Louisiana

Grambling State University, Grambling	
Louisiana State University and A&M College, Baton Rouge	Southern University and A&M College, Baton Rouge
Louisiana Tech University, Ruston	
University of New Orleans, New Orleans	Dillard University, New Orleans Louisiana State University Medical Center, New Orleans Loyola University, New Orleans Our Lady of Holy Cross College, New Orleans Southern University, New Orleans Tulane University, New Orleans Xavier University of Louisiana, New Orleans
University of Southwestern Louisiana, Lafayette	

Maine

| University of Maine, Orono | Husson College, Bangor |

| HOST COLLEGES | CROSS-ENROLLMENTS |

Maryland

| University of Maryland, College Park | Anne Arundel Community College, Arnold
Bowie State College, Bowie
George Mason University, Fairfax (VA)
Johns Hopkins University, Baltimore
Loyola College, Baltimore
Shepherd College, Shepherdstown (WV)
Towson State University, Towson
Western Maryland College, Westminster |

Massachusetts

Boston University, Boston	Northeastern University, Boston
College of the Holy Cross, Worcester	Anna Maria College, Paxton Assumption College, Worcester Becker Junior College, Leicester Becker Junior College, Worcester Central New England College, Worcester Clark University, Worcester Quinsigamond Community College, Worcester Worcester Polytechnic Institute, Worcester Worcester State College, Worcester
Massachusetts Institute of Technology, Cambridge	Harvard University, Cambridge Tufts University, Medford Wellesley College, Wellesley
University of Lowell, Lowell	Bentley College, Waltham Daniel Webster College, Nashua (NH) Endicott College, Beverly Gordon College, Wenham Middlesex Community College, Bedford New England College, Henniker (NH) New Hampshire College, Manchester (NH) Northern Essex Community College, Haverhill

HOST COLLEGES	CROSS-ENROLLMENTS

Massachusetts (continued)

	North Shore Community College, Beverly Notre Dame College, Manchester (NH) Rivier College, Nashua (NH) Saint Anselm College, Manchester (NH) Salem State College, Salem
University of Massachusetts, Amherst	Amherst College, Amherst Mount Holyoke College, South Hadley Smith College, Northampton Western New England College, Springfield

Michigan

Michigan State University, East Lansing	Lansing Community College, Lansing
Michigan Technological University, Houghton	Suomi College, Hancock
University of Michigan, Ann Arbor	Concordia College, Ann Arbor Eastern Michigan University, Ypsilanti Lawrence Institute of Technology, Southfield University of Michigan, Dearborn Wayne State University, Detroit

Minnesota

College of St Thomas, St Paul	Anoka-Ramsey Community College, Coon Rapids Augsburg College, Minneapolis Bethel College, St Paul College of St Catherine, St Paul Hamline University, St Paul Inver Hills Community College, Inver Grove Heights Lakewood Community College, White Bear Lake Macalester College, St Paul Normandale Community College, Bloomington North Hennepin Community College, Minneapolis

HOST COLLEGES	CROSS-ENROLLMENTS

Minnesota (continued)

	William Mitchell College of Law, St. Paul
University of Minnesota, Duluth	College of St Scholastica, Duluth
University of Minnesota, Minneapolis	

Mississippi

Mississippi State University, Mississippi State	Mississippi University for Women, Columbus
Mississippi Valley State University, Itta Bena	Delta State University, Cleveland
University of Mississippi, University	
University of Southern Mississippi, Hattiesburg	William Carey College, Hattiesburg

Missouri

Southeast Missouri State University, Cape Girardeau	
University of Missouri, Columbia	Columbia College, Columbia Stephens College, Columbia William Woods College, Fulton
University of Missouri, Rolla	

Montana

Montana State University, Bozeman	

Nebraska

University of Nebraska, Lincoln	Concordia Teachers College, Seward Nebraska Wesleyan University, Lincoln
University of Nebraska, Omaha	Bellevue College, Bellevue College of Saint Mary, Omaha Creighton University, Omaha Iowa Western Community College, Council Bluffs (IA) University of Nebraska Medical Center, Omaha

New Hampshire

University of New Hampshire, Durham	New England College, Henniker

HOST COLLEGES	CROSS-ENROLLMENTS

New Hampshire (continued)

	New Hampshire College, Manchester Plymouth State College, Plymouth Saint Anselm College, Manchester University of Southern Maine, Portland (ME)

New Jersey

New Jersey Institute of Technology, Newark	Essex County College, Newark Fairleigh Dickinson University, Teaneck Jersey City State College, Jersey City Kean College of New Jersey, Union Montclair State College, Upper Montclair Rutgers University, Newark Saint Peter's College, Jersey City Seton Hall University, South Orange Stevens Institute of Technology, Hoboken William Paterson College of New Jersey, Wayne
Rutgers University, New Brunswick	Brookdale Community College, Lincroft Mercer County Community College, West Windsor Middlesex County College, Edison Monmouth College, West Long Branch Princeton University, Princeton Rider College, Lawrenceville Rutgers University, Camden Somerset County College, Somerville Trenton State College, Trenton Union County College, Cranford Wagner College, Staten Island (NY)

New Mexico

New Mexico State University, Las Cruces	University of Texas, El Paso (TX)
University of New Mexico, Albuquerque	University of Albuquerque, Albuquerque

HOST COLLEGES	CROSS-ENROLLMENTS

New York

Clarkson University, Potsdam	St Lawrence University, Canton SUNY A&T College, Canton SUNY College, Potsdam
Cornell University, Ithaca	Ithaca College, Ithaca SUNY College, Cortland Tompkins Cortland Community College, Dryden Wells College, Aurora

Manhattan College, Riverdale	Academy of Aeronautics, Flushing
	Adelphi University, Garden City
	College of Mount Saint Vincent,
	    Riverdale
	Columbia University, New York
	Dowling College, Oakdale
	Elizabeth Seton College, Yonkers
	Long Island University, Brooklyn
	    Campus, Brooklyn
	Long Island University, C W Post
	    Campus, Greenvale
	Mercy College, Dobbs Ferry
	Molloy College, Rockville Centre
	Nassau Community College,
	    Garden City
	New York Institute of Technology,
	    Old Westbury
	Pace University, New York
	Polytechnic Institute of New York,
	    Brooklyn
	St Francis College, Brooklyn
	St Joseph's College, Patchogue
	St Thomas Aquinas College, Sparkill
	Southampton Community College,
	    Southampton
	Suffolk County Community College,
	    Brentwood
	SUNY A&T College, Farmingdale
	SUNY College, Old Westbury
	SUNY, Stony Brook

Rensselaer Polytechnic Institute, Troy	Albany College of Pharmacy of Union University, Albany College of Saint Rose, Albany

HOST COLLEGES	CROSS-ENROLLMENTS

New York (continued)

| | Fulton-Montgomery Community College, Johnstown
Hudson Valley Community College, Troy
Maria College, Albany
Russell Sage College, Troy
Schenectady County Community College, Schenectady
Siena College, Loudonville
Skidmore College, Saratoga Springs
SUNY, Albany
SUNY Empire State College, Saratoga Springs
Union College, Schenectady |
| Syracuse University, Syracuse | Le Moyne College, Syracuse
New School for Social Research, New York
Onondaga Community College, Syracuse
SUNY College of Environmental Science and Forestry, Syracuse
Utica College of Syracuse University, Utica |

North Carolina

Duke University, Durham	North Carolina Central University, Durham
East Carolina University, Greenville	Pitt Community College, Greenville
Fayetteville State University, Fayetteville	Pembroke State University, Pembroke
North Carolina A&T State University, Greensboro	Bennett College, Greensboro Greensboro College, Greensboro Guilford College, Greensboro High Point College, High Point University of North Carolina, Greensboro
North Carolina State University, Raleigh	Meredith College, Raleigh Peace College, Raleigh Saint Augustine's College, Raleigh St Mary's College, Raleigh Shaw University, Raleigh

HOST COLLEGES	CROSS-ENROLLMENTS

North Carolina (continued)

University of North Carolina, Chapel Hill	
University of North Carolina, Charlotte	Barber-Scotia College, Concord
	Belmont Abbey College, Belmont
	Central Piedmont Community College, Charlotte
	Davidson College, Davidson
	Gaston College, Dallas
	Johnson C Smith University, Charlotte
	Queens College, Charlotte
	Sacred Heart College, Belmont
	Wingate College, Wingate
	Winthrop College, Rock Hill (SC)

North Dakota

North Dakota State University, Fargo	Concordia College, Moorhead (MN)
	Moorhead State University, Moorhead (MN)

Ohio

Bowling Green State University, Bowling Green	Ashland College, Ashland
	Defiance College, Defiance
	Findlay College, Findlay
	Heidelberg College, Tiffin
	Ohio Northern University, Ada
	University of Toledo, Toledo
Kent State University, Kent	
Miami University, Oxford	Miami University, Hamilton
	Miami University, Middletown
Ohio State University, Columbus	Capital University, Columbus
	DeVry Institute of Technology, Columbus
	Franklin University, Columbus
	Ohio Dominican College, Columbus
	Ohio Wesleyan University, Delaware
	Otterbein College, Westerville
Ohio University, Athens	
University of Akron, Akron	

HOST COLLEGES	CROSS-ENROLLMENTS

Ohio (continued)

HOST COLLEGES	CROSS-ENROLLMENTS
University of Cincinnati, Cincinnati	Cincinnati Technical College, Cincinnati College of Mount St Joseph on the Ohio, Mount St Joseph Edgecliff College, Cincinnati Northern Kentucky University, Highland Heights (KY) Thomas More College, Crestview Hills (KY) Xavier University, Cincinnati
Wright State University, Dayton	Antioch College, Yellow Springs Cedarville College, Cedarville Central State University, Wilberforce Clark Technical College, Springfield Edison State Community College, Piqua Sinclair Community College, Dayton Southern State Community College, Hillsboro University of Dayton, Dayton Urbana University, Urbana Wilberforce University, Wilberforce Wilmington College of Ohio, Wilmington Wittenberg University, Springfield

Oklahoma

HOST COLLEGES	CROSS-ENROLLMENTS
Oklahoma State University, Stillwater	
University of Oklahoma, Norman	Oklahoma Christian College, Oklahoma City Oklahoma City University, Oklahoma City Rose State College, Midwest City St Gregory's College, Shawnee

Oregon

HOST COLLEGES	CROSS-ENROLLMENTS
Oregon State University, Corvallis	Linn-Benton Community College, Albany University of Oregon, Eugene Western Oregon State College, Monmouth

HOST COLLEGES	CROSS-ENROLLMENTS

Oregon (continued)

University of Portland, Portland	Clackamas Community College, Oregon City
	Clark College, Vancouver (WA)
	Concordia College, Portland
	Mt Hood Community College, Gresham
	Oregon Health Sciences University, Portland
	Portland Community College, Portland
	Portland State University, Portland
	Warner Pacific College, Portland
	Willamette University, Salem

Pennsylvania

Carnegie-Mellon University, Pittsburgh	
Grove City College, Grove City	Slippery Rock University of Pennsylvania, Slippery Rock
Lehigh University, Bethlehem	Allentown College of St Francis de Sales, Center Valley
	Cedar Crest College, Allentown
	East Stroudsburg University of Pennsylvania, East Stroudsburg
	Kutztown University of Pennsylvania, Kutztown
	Lafayette College, Easton
	Lehigh County Community College, Schnecksville
	Moravian College, Bethlehem
	Muhlenberg College, Allentown
	Northampton County Area Community College, Bethlehem
	Pennsylvania State University, Fogelsville
	Pennsylvania State University, Reading
Pennsylvania State University, University Park	
Saint Joseph's University, Philadelphia	Drexel University, Philadelphia
	Eastern College, St Davids
	La Salle University, Philadelphia
	Rutgers University, Camden (NJ)

HOST COLLEGES	CROSS-ENROLLMENTS

Pennsylvania (continued)

	Temple University, Philadelphia
	Thomas Jefferson University, Philadelphia
	University of Pennsylvania, Philadelphia
	Villanova University, Villanova
	West Chester University of Pennsylvania, West Chester
	Widener University, Chester
University of Pittsburgh, Pittsburgh	Carlow College, Pittsburgh
	Chatham College, Pittsburgh
	Community College of Allegheny County—Allegheny Campus, Pittsburgh
	Community College of Allegheny County—Boyce Campus, Monroeville
	Community College of Allegheny County—College Center North, Pittsburgh
	Community College of Allegheny County—South Campus, West Mifflin
	Duquesne University, Pittsburgh
	La Roche College, Pittsburgh
	Point Park College, Pittsburgh
	Robert Morris College, Coraopolis
	Saint Vincent College, Latrobe
Wilkes College, Wilkes-Barre	Bloomsburg University of Pennsylvania, Bloomsburg
	College Misericordia, Dallas
	Keystone Junior College, La Plume
	King's College, Wilkes-Barre
	Lackawanna Junior College, Scranton
	Luzerne County Community College, Nanticoke
	Marywood College, Scranton
	Pennsylvania State University, Dunmore
	Pennsylvania State University, Hazelton

HOST COLLEGES	CROSS-ENROLLMENTS
Pennsylvania (continued)	
	Pennsylvania State University, Wilkes-Barre
	University of Scranton, Scranton

Puerto Rico

University of Puerto Rico, Mayagüez	Inter American University of Puerto Rico, San Germán
	University of Puerto Rico, Ramey
University of Puerto Rico, Río Piedras	Bayamón Central University, Bayamón
	Bayamón Regional College, Río Piedras
	Inter American University of Puerto Rico, Hato Rey
	International Institute of the Americas of World University, Hato Rey
	University of Puerto Rico, Bayamón Technical University College, Bayamón
	University of Puerto Rico, Carolina Regional College, Carolina
	University of Puerto Rico, Cayey University College, Cayey
	University of Puerto Rico, Humacao University College, Humacao
	University of the Sacred Heart, Santurce

South Carolina

Baptist College at Charleston, Charleston	College of Charleston, Charleston
	Medical University of South Carolina, Charleston
	South Carolina State College, Orangeburg
The Citadel, Charleston (men only)	Central Wesleyan College, Central
Clemson University, Clemson	Anderson College, Anderson
	Greenville Technical College, Greenville
	Tri-County Technical College, Pendleton

HOST COLLEGES	CROSS-ENROLLMENTS

South Carolina (continued)

University of South Carolina, Columbia	Benedict College, Columbia

South Dakota

South Dakota State University, Brookings	

Tennessee

Memphis State University, Memphis	Christian Brothers College, Memphis LeMoyne-Owen College, Memphis Rhodes College, Memphis Shelby State Community College, Memphis University of Tennessee Center for the Health Sciences, Memphis
Tennessee State University, Nashville	Aquinas Junior College, Nashville Belmont College, Nashville David Lipscomb College, Nashville Fisk University, Nashville Meharry Medical College, Nashville Middle Tennessee State University, Murfreesboro Trevecca Nazarene College, Nashville Vanderbilt University, Nashville Volunteer State Community College, Gallatin Western Kentucky University, Bowling Green (KY)
University of Tennessee, Knoxville	Knoxville College, Knoxville

Texas

Angelo State University, San Angelo	
Baylor University, Waco	McLennan Community College, Waco Paul Quinn College, Waco University of Mary Hardin-Baylor, Belton
East Texas State University, Commerce	
North Texas State University, Denton	Southern Methodist University, Dallas Texas Woman's University, Denton University of Dallas, Irving University of Texas, Richardson

HOST COLLEGES	CROSS-ENROLLMENTS

Texas (continued)

HOST COLLEGES	CROSS-ENROLLMENTS
Southwest Texas State University, San Marcos	Texas Lutheran College, Seguin University of Texas, San Antonio
Texas A&M University, College Station	
Texas Christian University, Fort Worth	Baylor School of Nursing, Dallas Tarrant County Junior College, Fort Worth Texas Wesleyan College, Fort Worth University of Texas, Arlington
Texas Tech University, Lubbock	Lubbock Christian College, Lubbock
University of Texas, Austin	Austin Community College, Austin Concordia Lutheran College, Austin St Edward's University, Austin

Utah

Brigham Young University, Provo	Utah Technical College, Provo
University of Utah, Salt Lake City	Weber State College, Ogden Westminster College, Salt Lake City
Utah State University, Logan	

Vermont

Norwich University, The Military College of Vermont, Northfield	
Saint Michael's College, Winooski	Champlain College, Burlington Lyndon State College, Lyndonville Trinity College, Burlington University of Vermont, Burlington

Virginia

University of Virginia, Charlottesville	Piedmont Virginia Community College, Charlottesville
Virginia Military Institute, Lexington (men only)	
Virginia Polytechnic Institute and State University, Blacksburg	

Washington

Central Washington University, Ellensburg	

HOST COLLEGES	CROSS-ENROLLMENTS

Washington (continued)

University of Puget Sound, Tacoma	Fort Steilacoom Community College, Tacoma Pacific Lutheran University, Tacoma Saint Martin's College, Lacey Southern Illinois University, McChord AFB Tacoma Community College, Tacoma
University of Washington, Seattle	Bellevue Community College, Bellevue Edmonds Community College, Lynnwood Everett Community College, Everett Green River Community College, Auburn Highline Community College, Midway North Seattle Community College, Seattle Seattle Central Community College, Seattle Seattle University, Seattle Shoreline Community College, Seattle South Seattle Community College, Seattle
Washington State University, Pullman	University of Idaho, Moscow (ID)

West Virginia

West Virginia University, Morgantown	Fairmont State College, Fairmont

Wisconsin

University of Wisconsin, Madison	
University of Wisconsin, Superior	

Wyoming

University of Wyoming, Laramie	

E

Military Pay and Benefits

OFFICERS' YEARLY PAY

					Grade/Rank					
	O-1	O-2	O-3	O-4	O-5	O-6	O-7	O-8	O-9	O-10
ARMY/AIR FORCE/ MARINE CORPS	2nd Lieut	1st Lieut	Capt	Major	Lieut Colonel	Colonel	Brig General	Major General	Lieut General	General
NAVY/ COAST GUARD	Ensign	Lieut JG	Lieut	Lieut CDR	CDR	Capt	Commo	Rear Admiral	Vice Admiral	Admiral
Years of Service										
<2	$19,446	$22,032	$25,164	$27,612	$31,956	$38,532	$49,788	$58,044	$63,120	$70,032
2	20,016	23,544	27,384	32,016	36,144	41,508	52,536	59,496	64,536	72,180
3	23,100	27,156	28,848	33,672	38,088	43,668	52,536	60,696	65,712	72,180
4	23,100	27,888	31,236	33,672	38,088	43,668	52,536	60,696	65,712	72,180
6	23,100	28,356	32,436	34,152	38,088	43,668	54,480	60,696	65,712	72,180
8	23,100	28,356	33,372	35,340	38,088	43,668	54,480	64,536	67,140	74,592
10	23,100	28,356	34,836	37,248	39,012	43,668	57,108	64,536	67,140	74,592
14	23,100	28,356	36,984	40,380	42,876	44,868	59,496	67,140	69,564	77,904
20	23,100	28,356	36,984	42,780	48,852	53,736	68,328	74,529	77,904	77,904

Notes: 1. These rates are as of Jan. 1, 1985.

2. There are pay raises at 12, 16, 18, and over 20 years that have not been included.

3. The yearly pay shown includes base pay and a typical food allotment and housing allowance. The food allotment and housing allowance can vary depending on such factors as whether base housing and meals are provided.

4. There is additional pay for serving in high-cost-of-living areas and hazardous duty assignments.

Lieut = Lieutenant
Capt = Captain
Brig = Brigadier
JG = Junior Grade
CDR = Commander
Commo = Commodore

ENLISTED YEARLY PAY

Grade

Years of Service	E-1	E-2	E-3	E-4	E-5	E-6	E-7	E-8	E-9
<2	$12,360	$13,260	$13,596	$14,376	$15,528	$17,352	$19,608	—	—
2	12,360	13,260	14,064	14,892	16,404	18,372	20,640	—	—
3	12,360	13,260	14,436	15,468	16,920	18,876	21,168	—	—
4	12,360	13,260	14,820	16,272	17,412	19,428	21,672	—	—
6	12,360	13,260	14,820	16,704	18,180	19,920	22,200	—	—
8	12,360	13,260	14,820	16,704	18,684	20,424	22,692	$25,584	—
10	12,360	13,260	14,820	16,704	19,212	20,952	23,208	26,112	$29,544
14	12,360	13,260	14,820	16,704	19,968	22,200	24,504	27,132	30,564
20	12,360	13,260	14,820	16,704	19,968	22,968	25,788	28,668	32,112

Notes: 1. These rates are as of Jan. 1, 1985.

2. There are pay raises at 12, 16, 18, and over 20 years that have not been included.

3. The yearly pay shown includes base pay and a typical food allotment and housing allowance. The food allotment and housing allowance can vary depending on such factors as whether base housing and meals are provided.

4. There is additional pay for serving in high-cost-of-living areas and hazardous duty assignments.

OFFICER AND ENLISTED BENEFITS

In addition to their pay, military personnel receive substantial benefits. These include:

- Retirement. You may retire after twenty years and receive 50% of your base pay for the rest of your life. There is no contribution on your part to this retirement plan.

- Medical Care. You receive full medical and dental coverage at no charge. Most health care costs for your family are also covered.

- Life Insurance. If you die while on active duty your survivors are eligible for life insurance and other payments.

- Commissary and Exchange. These are military stores where you can buy food and other merchandise. On the average, costs are about 20% below civilian stores.

- Education. There are reduced rates for courses taken while on active duty, and the New GI Bill provides college money after you leave the service. Part II of this book explains these programs.

- Social and Recreational. Military bases provide child care centers, movie theaters, golf courses, and similar activities for a much lower cost than you would pay as a civilian.

- Travel. You may travel on military passenger aircraft for free when there is space available.

- Vacation. You have 30 days of leave, or vacation, each year.

Height and Weight Chart for Officers

As an example of a typical height and weight chart for all military officer programs, here is the one for the Army. This chart holds up fairly well for all six services except as noted below.

HEIGHT (in inches)	WEIGHT For Men (in lbs.)	WEIGHT For Women (in lbs.)
58		90–120
59		92–122
60	100–158	94–124
61	102–163	96–128
62	103–168	98–130
63	104–174	100–132
64	105–179	102–135
65	106–185	104–138
66	107–191	106–141
67	111–197	109–145
68	115–203	112–150
69	119–209	115–154
70	123–215	118–158
71	127–221	122–162
72	131–227	125–167
73	135–233	128–172
74	139–240	
75	143–246	
76	147–253	
77	151–260	
78	153–267	
79	159–273	
80	166–280	

NOTES:

1. For men: This chart is good for the Army, Navy, Marine Corps, and Merchant Marine. For the Air Force and Coast Guard, the upper weight limits are lighter, averaging about 10 pounds less for those who are 5'0" to 5'4" and about 20 pounds less for those who are 5'5" to 6'8".
2. For women: This chart is good for the Army. For the Navy, Air Force, Marine Corps, Coast Guard, and Merchant Marine, the upper weight limits are 6 pounds heavier.

Have You Seen These Other
Publications from Peterson's Guides?

Winning Money for College:
The High School Student's Guide to Scholarship
Contests
Alan Deutschman

The first complete guide to scholarship competitions that students can enter and win on their own. It is the only compilation of facts, figures, dates, and advice pertaining to America's most prestigious—and most financially rewarding—privately offered scholarships. Includes over 50 national contests that cover public speaking, science, citizenship, and more.

6" x 9", 220 pages   Stock no. 2618
ISBN 0-87866-261-8   **$7.95** paperback

The College Money Handbook 1986:
The Complete Guide to Expenses, Scholarships,
Loans, Jobs, and Special Aid Programs at Four-
Year Colleges
THIRD EDITION
Editor: Andrea E. Lehman
Data Editor: Eric A. Suber

The only book that describes the complete picture of costs and financial aid at accredited four-year colleges in the United States. The book is divided into three sections: an overview of the financial aid process and ways to make it work for you; cost and aid profiles of each college, showing need-based and non-need scholarship programs available; and directories listing colleges by the types of financial aid programs they offer.

8½" x 11", about 550 pages   Stock no. 3711
ISBN 0-87866-371-1   **$12.95** paperback

Peterson's Annual Guides/Undergraduate Study
Guide to Two-Year Colleges 1986
SIXTEENTH EDITION
Editor: Andrea E. Lehman
Data Editor: Eric A. Suber

This Guide covers nearly 1,450 accredited U.S. institutions that grant associate degrees. It contains basic college profiles, 1,800-word college essays written by admissions directors who chose to provide in-depth information, and directories of colleges by geographical area and by major. It serves as a companion volume to the *Guide to Four-Year Colleges 1986*.

8½" x 11", about 460 pages   Stock no. 3401
ISBN 0-87866-340-1   **$9.95** paperback

Peterson's Annual Guides/Undergraduate Study
Guide to Four-Year Colleges 1986
SIXTEENTH EDITION
Editor: Andrea E. Lehman
Data Editor: Eric A. Suber

The largest, most up-to-date guide to the over 1,900 accredited four-year colleges in the United States and Canada. Contains concise college profiles, a reader guidance section, and two-page "Messages from the Colleges" that are found in no other guide.

8½" x 11", 2,239 pages   Stock no. 3398
ISBN 0-87866-339-8   **$12.95** paperback

Peterson's Guide to College Admissions:
Getting into the College of Your Choice
THIRD EDITION
R. Fred Zuker and Karen C. Hegener

This updated edition takes students behind the scenes at college admissions offices and gives current advice from admissions directors all across the country. Contains dozens of campus photos and capsule profiles of 1,700 four-year colleges.

8½" x 11", 366 pages   Stock no. 2243
ISBN 0-87866-224-3   **$9.95** paperback

College 101
Dr. Ronald T. Farrar

The first book to answer the questions college-bound students most often ask—about money, health, social life, sex, and academic concerns. Written with empathy, common sense, and knowledge, this book can serve as a springboard to frank discussions of all college-related topics.

6" x 9", 177 pages   Stock no. 2693
ISBN 0-87866-269-3   **$6.95** paperback

Peterson's Guide to Colleges with Programs for
Learning-Disabled Students
Editors: Charles T. Mangrum II, Ed.D., and
     Stephen S. Strichart, Ph.D.

The most comprehensive guide available helps learning-disabled students find colleges that offer programs designed especially for them. Profiles of over 250 four-year colleges give general information about each college, detailed information on the learning-disabled programs each offers, and an easy-to-use Key Features Chart that summarizes the main features of the programs.

8½" x 11", about 400 pages   Stock no. 3274
ISBN 0-87866-327-4   **$13.95** paperback

Summer Jobs:
Finding Them, Getting Them, Enjoying Them
Sandra Schocket

Designed especially for high school and college students, this valuable guide shows how to find and get good summer jobs. It covers topics such as the process of finding a summer job, specific fields of employment that have summer jobs for students, options for students who want nontraditional types of employment (volunteer work, internships, working abroad, self-employment), and additional resources that might aid students in their summer job search.

6" x 9", 170 pages   Stock no. 3258
ISBN 0-87866-325-8   **$5.95** paperback

The Athlete's Game Plan for College and Career
Stephen Figler and Howard Figler

The first book to deal with *all* the commitments of a student athlete—academic achievement, athletic responsibilities, and career selection—and to show how to keep them in balance. Covers college selection, dealing with recruiters, financial aid, eligibility for college sports, study skills, coping strategies, education and athletics as bridges to career success, and job-hunting techniques.

6" x 9", 279 pages Stock no. 2669
ISBN 0-87866-266-9 **$9.95** paperback

How to Order

These publications are available from all good booksellers, or you may order direct from **Peterson's Guides, Dept. 5606, P.O. Box 2123, Princeton, New Jersey 08540.** Please note that prices are necessarily subject to change without notice.

- Enclose full payment for each book, plus postage and handling charges as follows:

Amount of Order	4th-Class Postage and Handling Charges
$1–$10	$1.25
$10.01–$20	$2.00
$20.01–$40	$3.00
$40.01 +	Add $1.00 shipping and handling for every additional $20 worth of books ordered.

Place your order TOLL-FREE by calling 800-225-0261 between 8:30 A.M. and 4:30 P.M. Eastern time, Monday through Friday. From New Jersey, Alaska, Hawaii, and outside the United States, call 609-924-5338. Telephone orders over $15 may be charged to your charge card; institutional and trade orders over $20 may be billed.

- For faster shipment via United Parcel Service (UPS), add $2.00 over and above the appropriate fourth-class book-rate charges listed.
- Bookstores and tax-exempt organizations should contact us for appropriate discounts.
- You may charge your order to VISA, MasterCard, or American Express. Minimum charge order: $15. Please include the name, account number, and validation and expiration dates for charge orders.
- New Jersey residents should add 6% sales tax to the cost of the books, excluding the postage and handling charge.
- Write for a free catalog describing all of our latest publications.